Biz
COMMON SENSE

Rachel Somer

ENTRY LEVEL

DARAKWON

Biz
COMMON
SENSE ENTRY LEVEL

Author Rachel Somer
Publisher Chung Kyudo
Editors Kwak Bitna, Cho Sangik
Designers Park Bohee, Lee Seunghyun
Photo Credit pg. 18 (road) ThirdFloorDraft; pg. 26 (baggage claim) Tooykrub, (currency exchange booth) Kenishirotie, (customs) RWicaksono, (arrivals) PokkO, (departures) Ververidis Vasilis, (duty-free shop) Song_about_summer, (immigration) Bale.P, (terminal) olrat, (check-in desk) Icatnews, (gate) ShutterStockStudio, (car rental booth) Kekyalyaynen; pg. 66 (tablet) bfk; pg. 90 (charity event) Jane Rix, (fundraiser) gnohz / Shutterstock.com

First Published April 2021
By Darakwon Inc.
Darakwon Bldg., 211, Munbal-ro, Paju-si, Gyeonggi-do 10881
Republic of Korea

Tel. 82-2-736-2031 (Ext. 552)

Price ₩14,000
ISBN 978-89-277-0987-9 14740
    978-89-277-0986-2 14740 (set)

http://www.darakwon.co.kr

Main Book / Free MP3 Available Online
7 6 5 4 3 2 1   21 22 23 24 25

Introduction

Biz Common Sense—12 Workplace Missions in English for Entry-level Professionals is designed for readers who wish to improve their English language skills for a professional environment. The book allows readers to experience situations that commonly occur on the job and provides meaningful guidance for responding to these situations.

The book is divided into twelve missions. Each mission includes three situations that focus on one typical scenario or problem that can occur in an entry-level business position. The situations are presented in a variety of formats, such as emails, conversations, telephone calls, voicemails, text messages, group chats, schedules, and notices.

Readers should begin each mission by reading Situation 1 and by answering some questions. This section is followed by background knowledge about the mission topic and a vocabulary exercise. Following that, readers practice a dialogue related to the topic and complete a one-page grammar lesson. Situation 2, which responds to Situation 1 with additional information, is presented next. Readers then learn a variety of relevant expressions before concluding the mission with Situation 3.

This book is ideal for classrooms, study groups, and individuals. Readers can complete the missions in any order they like. However, it is recommended that they complete all three situations in each mission before moving on. Completing each mission in full will give readers a greater understanding of problem-solving in an English-language workplace.

I would like to express my gratitude to Kwak Bitna, the editor of this book, as well as the entire Darakwon team. Their constant support made the development of this book possible.

I hope readers find this book useful in preparing them for real-world business situations. Solving problems in English can be overwhelming, but by studying the missions in this book, readers can gain the tools they need to feel confident in the workplace.

Rachel Somer

Scope and Sequence

Grammar	Expressions
The future tense	Making a request Responding to a suggestion
Prepositions of place	Asking for and giving directions Determining a current location Asking for clarification
The past simple tense	Explaining a cancelation Responding with sympathy Expressing gratitude
The present continuous tense	Making a suggestion Offering and asking for assistance
Should	Promising to do something Asking to be informed Providing assurance and reassurance
The future continuous tense	Relaying prior knowledge or instructions Expressing the necessity of an action Expressing certainty and approval

Grammar	Expressions
Gerunds after prepositions	Greeting someone formally and informally Responding to a greeting Interrupting someone
The passive voice	Asking about the possibility of an action Confirming and denying possibility and details Relaying details you are uncertain about
Wh-questions	Emphasizing an opinion or decision Understanding or finding out something Answering the phone Asking a customer to wait on the phone
Participle adjectives	Informing someone of a change of plans Expressing regret about a change of plans Encouraging someone to attend an event Apologizing for a serious disruption
It as an impersonal pronoun	Giving a customer instructions Highlighting a service or a feature Thanking a customer Ending a business email or letter
Imperative sentences	Explaining an action via email Asking that something be done via email Continuing a conversation Mentioning something is lost

Situation ❶

A Adrienne Smith's boss is going to have an important meeting and emails her to ask her to prepare for it. Read the email.

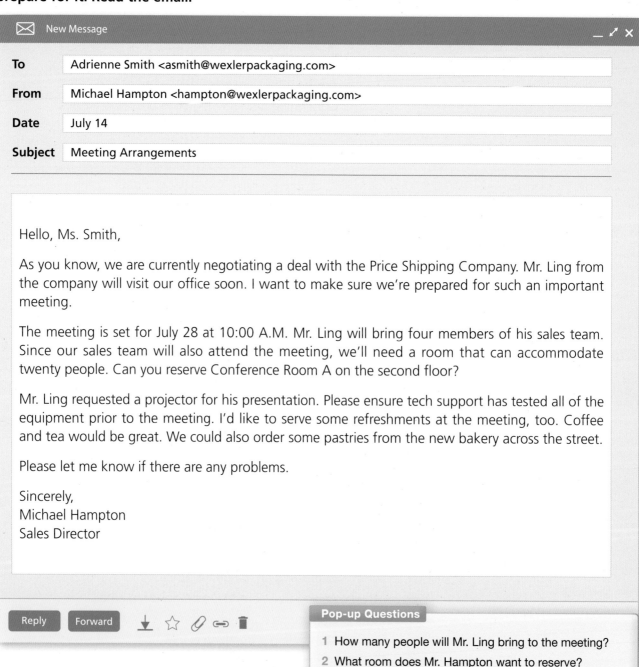

✉ New Message — ↗ ✕

To	Adrienne Smith <asmith@wexlerpackaging.com>
From	Michael Hampton <hampton@wexlerpackaging.com>
Date	July 14
Subject	Meeting Arrangements

Hello, Ms. Smith,

As you know, we are currently negotiating a deal with the Price Shipping Company. Mr. Ling from the company will visit our office soon. I want to make sure we're prepared for such an important meeting.

The meeting is set for July 28 at 10:00 A.M. Mr. Ling will bring four members of his sales team. Since our sales team will also attend the meeting, we'll need a room that can accommodate twenty people. Can you reserve Conference Room A on the second floor?

Mr. Ling requested a projector for his presentation. Please ensure tech support has tested all of the equipment prior to the meeting. I'd like to serve some refreshments at the meeting, too. Coffee and tea would be great. We could also order some pastries from the new bakery across the street.

Please let me know if there are any problems.

Sincerely,
Michael Hampton
Sales Director

Reply | Forward   ↓ ☆ 🖉 🔗 🗑

Pop-up Questions

1 How many people will Mr. Ling bring to the meeting?
2 What room does Mr. Hampton want to reserve?
3 What equipment did Mr. Ling request?
4 What does Mr. Hampton want to order from the bakery?

B Take Notes :: Based on the email in A, complete the memo.

Agenda: Negotiations with the [1] _____ Company

Date / Time: [2] _____

Place: [3] _____ Room A

Number of Attendees: [4] _____

To Do:

- The projector needs to be tested by [5] _____ .
- Refreshments: [6] _____ , [7] _____ , and [8] _____ from the new bakery

Background Knowledge

A Read and learn about types of meetings.

Meetings are an important part of doing business. People discuss many items related to business, such as sales figures, marketing plans, and budgets. There are many different ways to hold a meeting.

Face-to-face meetings are easy and effective. Workers in the same office can meet in a conference room. They might also meet at a restaurant or café. Sometimes people travel great distances just to meet colleagues in person.

Meetings can also happen over the phone. Phone meetings between two people are quite common. Conference calls are useful, too. Workers can discuss business from anywhere in the world during a conference call.

Video conferencing is becoming more and more popular. Some offices have video conferencing systems. Workers can call another team in another location. Video conferencing software can also be used on personal computers. People can conduct video conferences from the comfort of their homes.

Pop-up Questions

1 What do people discuss during meetings?

2 What type of meeting can happen at home?

B Listen to the conversation and answer the questions. 🔊 01-1

1 **Who is having a meeting next week?**

a. Jeff and Wanda   b. Jeff and Max   c. Jeff and Ms. West

2 **What type of meeting does Wanda suggest?**

a. a conference call   b. a video conference   c. an in-person meeting

3 **Where will the meeting likely happen?**

a. in the conference room   b. on the first floor   c. in Max's office

Vocabulary

A Look at the pictures and learn some words related to meetings.

Types of Meeting Rooms

conference room

theater

meeting booth

brainstorming area

Equipment for Meetings

projector and screen

laptop

whiteboard and markers

speaker

microphone

video-conferencing camera

monitor

speakerphone

B Complete the sentences with the words in the box.

| monitor | whiteboard and markers | speakers | microphone |
| video-conferencing camera | speakerphone | brainstorming area | theater |

1 The man is speaking into a _____ to make his voice louder.

2 We can't hear them because the _____ are not working.

3 The training video plays on the computer _____.

4 Let's go to the _____. There are comfortable chairs there.

5 The teams are having an international call using the _____.

6 He will give his presentation in the _____ because there are more chairs.

7 Turn on your _____. I can't see your face.

8 He draws the figures by using a _____.

10

Speak Up

Practice the conversation with your partner by using the information in each meeting plan. 01-2

Example

Meeting Type: in person

Meeting Room Type: the conference room

Number of Attendees: 12 people

Purpose: to discuss the yearly budget

Necessary Equipment: projector

Plan 1

Meeting Type: in person

Meeting Room Type: the theater

Number of Attendees: 32 people

Purpose: to present our marketing plan

Necessary Equipment: speakers

Plan 2

Meeting Type: virtual

Meeting Room Type: the conference room

Number of Attendees: two teams

Purpose: to talk about our sales figures

Necessary Equipment: video-conferencing system

Plan 3

Meeting Type: virtual

Meeting Room Type: the meeting booth

Number of Attendees: 3 people

Purpose: to plan the next training session

Necessary Equipment: laptop

A Hello. I need some help setting up a meeting.

B Sure. What's the meeting for?

A We're going to discuss the yearly budget.

B How many people will attend?

A There will be 12 people in total.

B Is it in person or virtual?

A I'd prefer it to be in person.

B Okay. So then you'll need to use the conference room.

A That's right. I want to make sure the projector is/are working.

B No problem. I will check if it's/they're working in advance.

Tips for Success

Your meeting will run smoothly with the right equipment. Ask tech support to check that it works before your meeting starts.

GRAMMAR

A **Let's learn about the future tense.**

will	be + going to + verb
Use **will + verb** to express an immediate voluntary action or **will not (won't) + verb** to make a negative sentence.	Use **be (not) + going to + verb** when you have made a decision to do or not to do something.
Mr. Ling **will visit** our office soon. He **will bring** four members of his team. The client **will not arrive** on time.	I **am going to apply** for the job. We **are going to attend** the conference. He **is not going to take** a vacation this year.

B **Complete the sentences by using the future tense forms of the verbs in parentheses.**

1 **A** I'm so exhausted. I didn't sleep well.

    B I _____ you some coffee from the breakroom. (*get*)

2 **A** Why do you need a notepad?

    B I _____ a memo to the receptionist. (*write*)

3 **A** I heard you are going on vacation with your family.

    B Yes, we _____ the Australian Outback. (*tour*)

4 **A** It's freezing in here! Oh, no. The heater is broken.

    B I _____ the Maintenance Department. (*call*)

5 **A** Did you hear the conference has been canceled?

    B That's too bad. I _____ my flight then. (*cancel*)

6 **A** What did you discuss in the budget meeting?

    B Well, we _____ anymore office equipment this year. (*not buy*)

📶 Know-how *at* Work   How to Reserve a Room

It is important to reserve meeting rooms in advance. Offices are busy places. Meetings are always happening. Reserving a room means that a space will be free exactly when you need it. There are a few steps to take.

1 Contact the person responsible for reservations. Mention the time and the date of your meeting. Ask about the rooms available during that time.

2 Make sure to mention how many people will be attending. Some meeting rooms may be too small. They might not have enough chairs. Choose a room that can accommodate your group.

3 Explain the equipment you will need for your meeting, such as projectors and computers. If your room doesn't have the right equipment, ask if it can be installed.

4 Contact tech support. Ask someone to check the equipment in your meeting room. Make sure it works prior to the meeting date. Request repairs for any broken equipment.

Situation 2

A Adrienne Smith makes a phone call to reserve one of the conference rooms in the building. Read the telephone conversation. 🔊 01-3

Adrienne Smith Hello. This is Adrienne Smith, the assistant to Michael Hampton, calling.

Wesley Simpson Hi, Ms. Smith. What can I do for you?

Adrienne Smith I'd like to reserve a room for July 28 at 10:00 A.M.

Wesley Simpson Sure. What room are you thinking of?

Adrienne Smith Mr. Hampton requested Conference Room A.

Wesley Simpson Okay, let me check the reservation schedule. Oh, that time slot was already booked by the Accounting Department.

Adrienne Smith That's too bad. Are there any other rooms available?

Wesley Simpson How many people are going to attend?

Adrienne Smith Twenty in total.

Wesley Simpson How about the theater on the first floor?

Adrienne Smith Hmm, I'm not sure Mr. Hampton will like that. The chairs should face one another so the teams can speak comfortably.

Wesley Simpson Well, Conference Room C is available. It only has fifteen chairs, but we can move more in.

Adrienne Smith That will have to do. Can you check if the projector works, too?

Wesley Simpson Sure, no problem!

Pop-up Questions

1 What is the problem with Conference Room A?
2 What room does Mr. Simpson suggest first?
3 What is the problem with Conference Room C?
4 What does Ms. Smith ask Mr. Simpson to check?

B **Problem Solving ::** Adrienne Smith gets a call from Wesley Simpson saying that her boss cannot use Conference Room C because the projector is not working. Find a partner and choose the roles of Adrienne Smith and Wesley Simpson. Then, role-play to discuss a possible solution. Use the information from the telephone conversation in A if necessary.

A **Let's learn some expressions to use in business.**

When making a polite request	When making an informal request
I'd like to reserve a room.	Can you check if the projector works?
I'm interested in applying for the course.	Could they switch rooms with us?
Would you mind sending it by email?	Will you close the window?
May I postpone the meeting?	Would you find some more chairs?
When a suggestion is not satisfactory	**When a suggestion is satisfactory**
I'm not sure he will like that.	That will have to do.
I don't think that will work.	I think that will work.
I'm not sure about that.	I think she will approve of that.
That might be a problem.	That will be fine.

B **Fill in the blanks with the correct answers from the box. Then, practice the conversation with a partner.** 01-4

can you check if the projector works	I'd like to reserve a room
that will have to do	I don't think that will work

A Hello. [1] _____ for next Friday.

B Sure, no problem. Which room?

A I'd like Conference Room 305 on the third floor.

B Okay, what time do you want to reserve it?

A From 10:00 until 11:30 A.M.

B That time has already been booked. How about from 11:30 to 1:00 P.M.?

A [2] _____. We have a company lunch planned then.

B Would you like to use Conference Room 303? It's the same size as 305.

A [3] _____.

B Okay, great. I'll add your name to the reservation schedule.

A Thanks. In addition, [4] _____?

Extra Practice

Role-play with your partner. One person requests a room. The other person suggests an alternate room.

A I'd like to reserve Conference Room 1010 for this Thursday.

B That room is booked this week.

A I see. Is room 3020 available?

B I think that will work.

Situation 3

Adrienne Smith gets an email from her boss the day after the meeting to let her know how it went. Read it and see if the results are positive or negative.

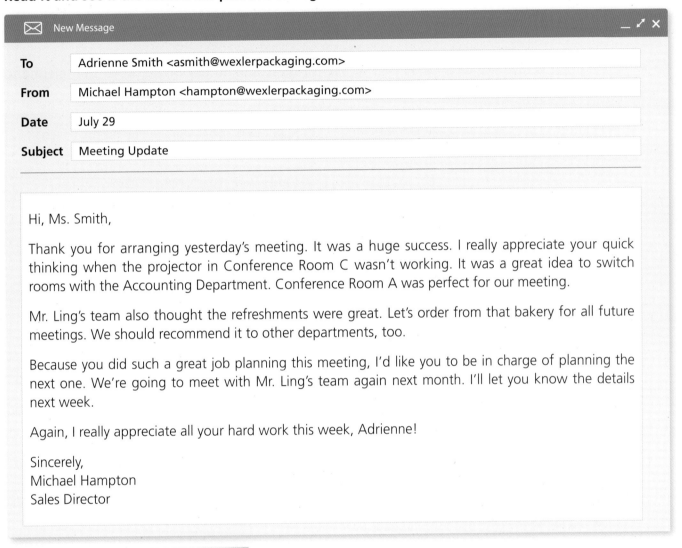

✉ New Message	— ↗ ✕
To	Adrienne Smith <asmith@wexlerpackaging.com>
From	Michael Hampton <hampton@wexlerpackaging.com>
Date	July 29
Subject	Meeting Update

Hi, Ms. Smith,

Thank you for arranging yesterday's meeting. It was a huge success. I really appreciate your quick thinking when the projector in Conference Room C wasn't working. It was a great idea to switch rooms with the Accounting Department. Conference Room A was perfect for our meeting.

Mr. Ling's team also thought the refreshments were great. Let's order from that bakery for all future meetings. We should recommend it to other departments, too.

Because you did such a great job planning this meeting, I'd like you to be in charge of planning the next one. We're going to meet with Mr. Ling's team again next month. I'll let you know the details next week.

Again, I really appreciate all your hard work this week, Adrienne!

Sincerely,
Michael Hampton
Sales Director

Business English Dos and Don'ts

When your coworkers or colleagues do an excellent job, you might have to thank them. Mention what it is you're thankful for. Be as specific as possible, especially in writing.

Dos	**Don'ts**
○ Thank you for arranging yesterday's meeting. (*specific*)	✕ Thanks a lot. (*too general*)
○ I really appreciate all your hard work this week. (*specific*)	✕ Thanks for that stuff. (*too general*)

Unless your coworkers or colleagues are also your friends, try not to use informal phrases.

Dos	**Don'ts**
○ On behalf of the company, I'd like to thank you. (*formal*)	✕ Thanks, dude! (*too casual*)
○ I'm very grateful for your help with this matter. (*formal*)	✕ Hey, thanks for your help. (*too casual*)

Situation ❶

A A deliveryman is lost and calls Cindy Bell to ask for directions to her office. Read the telephone conversation. 🔊 02-1

Max Judd This is Max from Speedy Delivery. I was on my way over with your delivery, but I seem to be lost.

Cindy Bell We're in a new building, so it sometimes doesn't show up on GPS.

Max Judd Could you give me directions?

Cindy Bell Sure. Where are you now?

Max Judd I'm currently parked on Baker Avenue in front of the Starview Department Store.

Cindy Bell I know where that is. First, go north three blocks. Then, turn right onto Clifford Road.

Max Judd Okay. How long do I stay on Clifford?

Cindy Bell About ten minutes. Clifford will take you straight to the waterfront. You'll see some warehouses on your left. Turn left there and drive past the docks.

Max Judd That will take me to the beach, right?

Cindy Bell That's right. There are a few restaurants and shops there. Our building is just past them.

Max Judd Let me double-check the address. You're at 145 Portside Lane?

Cindy Bell That's right. The building is the tallest in the area. You can't miss it!

Max Judd Great. Thanks for your help.

Pop-up Questions

1 Why doesn't Ms. Bell's building show up on GPS?
2 Where will Clifford Road take Mr. Judd?
3 What should Mr. Judd do when he sees the warehouses?
4 Why won't Mr. Judd miss Ms. Bell's building?

B Take Notes :: Based on the telephone conversation in A, summarize the directions.

First	Go north ¹_____ blocks.
Second	Turn ²_____ onto Clifford Road.
Third	Take Clifford Road to the ³_____.
Fourth	Turn ⁴_____ at the ⁵_____ and drive past the docks.
Fifth	Drive past the ⁶_____ and the shops.

Background Knowledge

A Read and learn about giving directions on streets.

Giving directions is an important tool when communicating. You might need to give directions to your workplace. You might also need to tell a colleague how to reach a restaurant, hotel, or airport. There are a few things to remember when giving directions.

First, determine the location of the person you are trying to help. Ask for the street name as well as any nearby stores or landmarks. If you know the area well, you can give verbal directions. Keep each direction short and concise. Use the words "left" and "right" when explaining turns. Mention important features, like rivers, mountains, or landmarks.

If you are not familiar with an area, try using a map. You can find maps online. Do a simple search and then use the map to give directions verbally. Additionally, you can take a screenshot of the map and send it by text message.

Pop-up Questions

1 What can you do if you know an area well when giving directions?

2 What can you send by text message when giving directions?

B Listen to the conversation and answer the questions. 🔊 02-2

1 **Who needs directions to the office?**

   a. Sally   b. Brandon   c. Robert

2 **What did the Plaza used to be?**

   a. a theater   b. a department store   c. an office

3 **What should the person do on First Avenue?**

   a. Turn left.   b. Turn right.   c. Go one block.

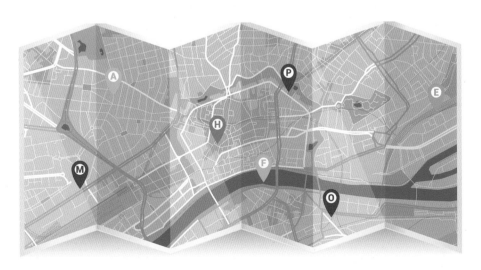

Vocabulary

A Look at the pictures and learn some words related to giving directions.

B Complete the sentences with the words in the box.

dead end	traffic circle	traffic light	waterfront
one-way street	crosswalk	alley	blocks

1 Stop your vehicle when the _____ is red.

2 We have to turn around. We've reached a(n) _____.

3 Cars on Baker Street can only drive west. It's a(n) _____.

4 The man stops at the _____ to enjoy the ocean.

5 Pedestrians should use the _____ when crossing the street.

6 Cars drive in a circle by using the _____.

7 The _____ is too narrow for cars. Please get out and walk.

8 To get to the office, go three _____ and then turn right.

Speak Up

Practice the conversation with your partner by using the information on each map. 02-3

A Hello. This is Steven calling. I'm on my way to your office, but I seem to be lost.

B I can give you directions. Where are you right now?

A I'm going north on First Street. I'm right by the car dealership.

B Keep going north. Then, turn right onto Queen Road.

A How long do I stay on Queen Road?

B Just a few minutes. Go past Carlton Street.

A Okay. Then what?

B You'll see a hospital on your left. Our office is across from it.

A Great. Thank you!

B No problem. If you see the bakery, you've gone too far.

Tips for Success

When giving directions, mention what is next to or across from the destination.

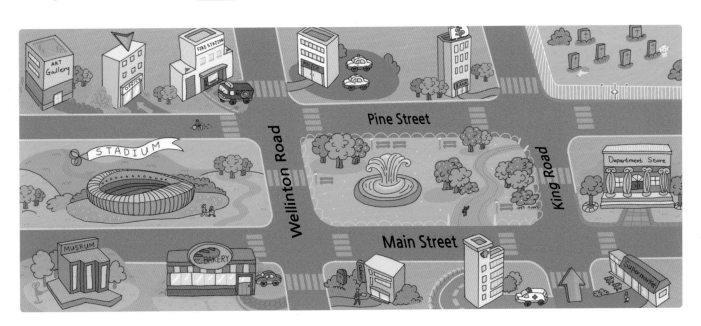

A Let's learn about giving directions by using prepositions of place.

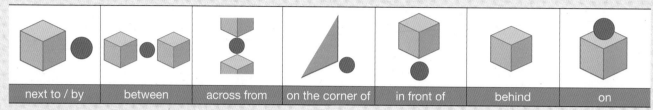

| next to / by | between | across from | on the corner of | in front of | behind | on |

The bakery is **next to** the department store.

The post office is **between** the museum and the bank.

The office is **across from** the fire station.

The park is **on the corner of** King Street and Stevenson Road.

The parking lot is **in front of** the stadium.

The supermarket is **behind** the hospital.

The police station is **on** West Street.

B Look at the map and write the correct prepositions in the blanks.

1 A Where is the department store?

  B It's _____ the bakery.

2 A Where is the park?

  B It's _____ Second Street.

3 A Where is the office?

  B It's _____ the flower shop.

4 A Where is the bank?

  B It's _____ Fall Avenue and Second Street.

5 A Where is the hospital?

  B It's _____ the school.

📶 Know-how at Work   **How to Arrange to Receive Deliveries**

Workplaces receive a lot of deliveries. Office supplies, product samples, and furniture are just a few examples of things delivered. Making arrangements can ensure you get your deliveries on time.

1   If you are expecting a delivery, make sure to answer your phone or to check your text messages. The delivery person may be trying to contact you.

2   Some buildings have receptionists or security guards in the lobby. Let them know if you're expecting a delivery. They can help the delivery person with any problems.

3   If there is construction or maintenance happening in the building, make alternate arrangements to receive deliveries. Let the delivery person know which door or elevator to use.

4   Some delivery companies ask you to sign for deliveries. If you're out of the office, ask another employee to sign for you.

Situation ②

Ⓐ Cindy Bell gets a text message from Max Judd, who is unable to use the elevator. Read the text message chain.

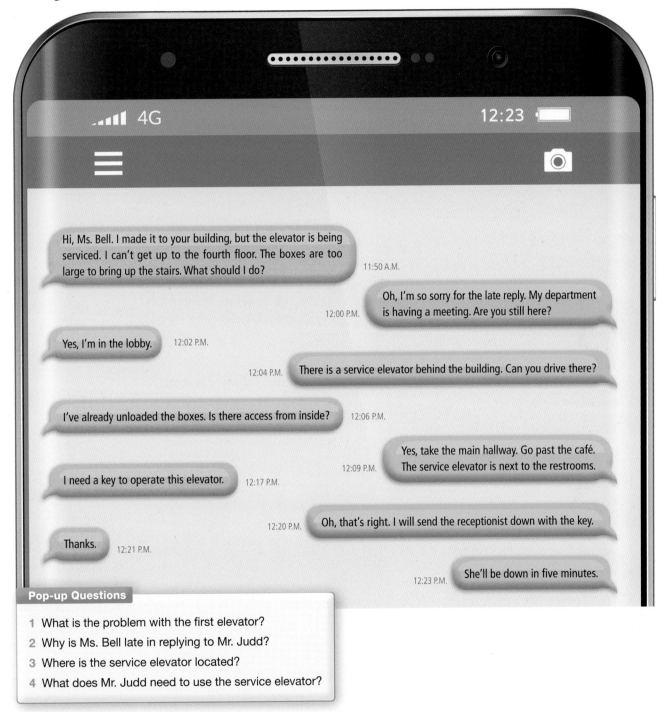

Hi, Ms. Bell. I made it to your building, but the elevator is being serviced. I can't get up to the fourth floor. The boxes are too large to bring up the stairs. What should I do? — 11:50 A.M.

12:00 P.M. — Oh, I'm so sorry for the late reply. My department is having a meeting. Are you still here?

Yes, I'm in the lobby. 12:02 P.M.

12:04 P.M. — There is a service elevator behind the building. Can you drive there?

I've already unloaded the boxes. Is there access from inside? 12:06 P.M.

12:09 P.M. — Yes, take the main hallway. Go past the café. The service elevator is next to the restrooms.

I need a key to operate this elevator. 12:17 P.M.

12:20 P.M. — Oh, that's right. I will send the receptionist down with the key.

Thanks. 12:21 P.M.

12:23 P.M. — She'll be down in five minutes.

Pop-up Questions

1 What is the problem with the first elevator?
2 Why is Ms. Bell late in replying to Mr. Judd?
3 Where is the service elevator located?
4 What does Mr. Judd need to use the service elevator?

Ⓑ Problem Solving :: Max Judd calls and tells Cindy Bell that the service elevator is out of order. Find a partner and choose the roles of Max Judd and Cindy Bell. Then, role-play to discuss a possible solution. Use the information from the text message chain in A if necessary.

Useful Expressions

A **Let's learn some expressions to use in business.**

When asking for directions	When determining a current location
Could you give me directions?	Where are you now?
Can you tell me how to get there?	What street are you on now?
Do you know where the waterfront is?	Are you near any landmarks?
Can you tell me what street to take?	What stores do you see now?
When giving directions	**When asking for clarification**
Take the main hallway and go past the café.	How long do I stay on Clifford?
Go north three blocks and turn left.	Which street do I turn onto?
First, turn left onto Pine Street.	Where will that take me?
Turn right onto Clifford Street.	What is it next to/across from/in front of?

B **Fill in the blanks with the correct answers from the box. Then, practice the conversation with a partner.** ◀》 02-4

Go south and turn right onto King Street	Which street do I turn onto
Where are you now	Could you give me directions

A Hello. This is Mandy from Marketing Solutions.

B Hi, Mandy. This is Tim. I'm on my way to your office, but I think I'm lost.

A I'm sorry to hear that. ¹ _____ ?

B I'm going south on Lake Street. ² _____ ?

A Sure. Are you near any landmarks?

B Well, I'm very close to the beach.

A Okay. ³ _____ .

B How long do I stay on King Street?

A About five minutes. Go past the hospital and turn left.

B ⁴ _____ ?

A First Street. My office is across from the park.

Extra Practice

Role-play with your partner. One person mentions he or she is lost. The other person gives some directions.

A I'm lost. Could you give me directions to your office?

B Sure. Go north on Baker Avenue three blocks. Then, turn right.

A Which street do I turn onto?

B Wellview Road. My office is next to the bank.

Situation ③

Cindy Bell gets a voicemail message from Max Judd explaining another problem with the elevators. Read it and see if the results are positive or negative. 🔊 02-5

You have one new message, sent at 12:50 P.M. on June 14.

Hello. This is Max Judd calling from Speedy Delivery. Your receptionist brought the key down, but the service elevator is out of order. I asked the workers repairing the main elevator. They said they cut the power to all the elevators in order to do the repairs.

Unfortunately, I had to leave your boxes in the lobby. They're next to the café you mentioned. Your receptionist said she can have someone move them later. The elevators won't be working again until the evening, and I'm already late with other deliveries.

Most buildings have security staff in the lobby to manage these types of problems. I'm not sure why this building doesn't.

Anyway, have a nice day.

Business English Dos and Don'ts

When you are giving directions, there are a few ways to makes sure the receiver understands you. Give clear, concise directions. Don't give too many directions at once.

Dos	**Don'ts**
○ Go three blocks. Then, turn left at the intersection. (*concise*)	✕ Drive for a few blocks and then make a turn. (*confusing*)
○ Take Bay Street to the waterfront. Then, turn right. (*concise*)	✕ Go under the overpass. Turn left, then turn right, and then turn left again. (*confusing*)

Mention famous landmarks or places the receiver knows.

Dos	**Don'ts**
○ They're next to the café you mentioned. (*clear*)	✕ It's beside one of the bus stops on Park Road. (*unclear*)
○ It's across from the Hargrave Theater. (*clear*)	✕ It's behind that new building downtown. (*unclear*)

Situation ①

A Kathy Sanchez's boss, Dan Johansen, contacts her to ask her to pick a client up at the airport. Read the voicemail messages. 🔊 03-1

You have one new message, sent at 1:45 P.M. on February 5.

Hi, Kathy. This is Dan from Management. I just want to remind you that Annabeth Sweet is flying in to discuss the distribution of her new clothing line.

As you know, Ms. Sweet is a very important client. I think it would be best if one of us picked her up at the airport personally. Would you be able to do that?

Ms. Sweet is departing London at 10:25 A.M. on February 7 on Flight ZF83 with Zanford Airlines. She'll arrive here in New York at 2:05 P.M. Let me know if you're available. Thanks, Kathy.

You have one new message, sent at 2:01 P.M. on February 5.

Hi, Kathy. This is Dan again. I think I may have given you the wrong arrival time. It's 1:05 P.M. It would be great if you could get there 30 minutes early. You can take one of the company cars. Thanks again!

Pop-up Questions

1 Why is Ms. Sweet flying in?
2 What date does Ms. Sweet depart London?
3 What city is Ms. Sweet flying to?
4 What information did Mr. Johansen get wrong?

B Take Notes :: Based on the voicemail messages in A, complete the itinerary.

Flight Itinerary

Passenger: Annabeth Sweet   *Airline:* Zanford Airlines
Departure Date: February 7

City of Departure	Flight	Departure Time	City of Arrival	Arrival Time
1	2	3	4	5

Background Knowledge

Ⓐ Read and learn about picking up clients at the airport.

When picking up clients at the airport, it's important to make a good impression. This means being punctual. You don't want to make your client wait for you. Check the client's itinerary in advance. Note the flight number and the arrival time. Try to get to the airport before the scheduled arrival time.

When you get to the airport, go to arrivals. There are different sections for domestic and international arrivals. Locate the one your client will be arriving at. If you've never met the client, you might not recognize him or her. Hold a sign with the client's name written on it.

Greet your client politely. Ask how the flight was and if there were any problems. Never complain about how long you had to wait. Offer to help carry the client's bags to the car. It's a good idea to keep some refreshments in the car. Offer your client some water or juice.

Pop-up Questions

1 What should you hold when meeting a client for the first time?

2 What should you offer to help your client carry?

Ⓑ Listen to the conversation and answer the questions. 🔊 03-2

1 **Who is picking up a client at the airport?**

   a. Steve   b. Jenny   c. Mr. Vangaras

2 **How early should someone arrive when picking up a client?**

   a. 30 minutes   b. an hour   c. two hours

3 **What is the last piece of advice?**

   a. to be punctual   b. to be friendly   c. to be smart

Vocabulary

A Look at the pictures and learn some places at an airport.

B Complete the sentences with the words in the box.

car rental booth	baggage claim	gate	duty-free shop
check-in desk	airport security	currency exchange booth	departures

1 The man is picking up his bags from _____.

2 Wait at the _____ to board your plane.

3 You can get your boarding pass at the _____.

4 For everyone's safety, passengers must go through _____.

5 Stacey is going to the _____ to rent a vehicle.

6 If you need local currency, go to the _____.

7 Please drop me off at _____. I'm leaving the country today.

8 Can you purchase some perfume at the _____?

Speak Up

Practice the conversation with your partner by using the information on each itinerary. 🔊 03-3

Example

Client's Name: Bella Santos

Reason for Delay: mechanical issues

Departure Time: 4:40 P.M.

City of Arrival: Toronto

Arrival Area: domestic

Arrival Time: 9:50 P.M.

Instructions: drive her to the Star Hotel

Itinerary 1

Client's Name: Christopher Arden

Reason for Delay: X

Departure Time: 8:05 A.M.

City of Arrival: Sydney

Arrival Area: international

Arrival Time: 6:35 P.M.

Instructions: take him to dinner at Gianni's Restaurant

Itinerary 2

Client's Name: Jin Hong

Reason for Delay: heavy snowfall

Departure Time: 11:20 A.M.

City of Arrival: Seoul

Arrival Area: international

Arrival Time: 2:40 P.M.

Instructions: bring him directly to the office

Itinerary 3

Client's Name: Sergei Ivanov

Reason for Delay: X

Departure Time: 7:00 A.M.

City of Arrival: Moscow

Arrival Area: domestic

Arrival Time: 11:15 A.M.

Instructions: take him to lunch at Anna's Café

A Did you pick up Bella Santos at the airport yesterday?

B Yes, I did.

A Was his/her flight delayed?

B No, it wasn't. / Yes, it was delayed due to mechanical issues.

A What was the departure time?

B It was 4:40 P.M.

A And what time did he/she arrive here in Toronto?

B It was a(n) domestic flight, so he/she arrived at 9:50 P.M.

A What did you do after picking him/her up?

B The manager asked me to drive her to the Star Hotel.

! **Tips for Success**

After picking up a client at the airport, you must drive the client to another location. Get the name of the hotel, restaurant, or café in advance.

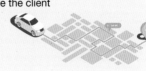

 **GRAMMAR**

A **Let's learn about the past simple tense.**

Regular	Irregular
Add **-ed** to regular verbs to show something happened in the past.	Irregular verbs take different forms.
asked, played, talked, called, decided	**found, heard, bought, spoke, broke, paid, drove**
My manager **asked** me to meet her at the restaurant. I **called** you yesterday to confirm your arrival time. We **decided** to delay the meeting time by an hour.	Yesterday, I **spoke** with his assistant. The company **bought** a new copy machine. Jessica **found** three extra chairs for the meeting.

B **Complete the sentences with the words in the box. Change the forms of the verbs to the past tense.**

break	pay	call	show	hear	ask	pick	drive

1 The demonstration was great. He _____ us all the new products.

2 This is Rita calling. I _____ from Tim that you are organizing the meeting.

3 Sam _____ the printer last week. It will be repaired on Friday.

4 I _____ for the items already. Can you send me a receipt?

5 Ms. West _____ for an 11:00 A.M. meeting. Will that work for you?

6 They _____ the colors for the company logo. I think they chose white and green.

7 Mr. Green _____ the client from the airport to her hotel yesterday.

8 I _____ you an hour ago, but you didn't answer. Were you busy?

Know-how *at* **Work**   **How to Respond to a Flight Delay**

Flight delays are common. Sometimes poor weather conditions delay a flight. Occasionally, there are mechanical issues with the plane. This can cause problems when a client needs to be picked up at the airport.

1　If you've hired a pickup service, call to inform the company of the delay. The company is likely aware of the situation, but it's a good idea to double-check.

2　If you are personally picking someone up, check the new arrival time. Plan to get to the airport about thirty minutes before that time.

3　Use airline or airport websites. They can provide you with updates about arrival times. They can inform you of further delays.

4　Be available if the client needs to contact you. Reassure the client that he or she will be picked up upon arrival despite the delay.

Situation ②

A Kathy Sanchez gets a phone call from the client informing her that the flight was delayed. Read the telephone conversation. 🔊 03-4

🕽 **Annabeth Sweet** Hi, Kathy Sanchez? This is Annabeth Sweet. I heard you are going to pick me up at the airport. So I thought I'd call you directly.

🕽 **Kathy Sanchez** Yes, that's right. Is there something I can help you with?

🕽 **Annabeth Sweet** Yes, actually, I just found out my flight has been delayed.

🕽 **Kathy Sanchez** Oh, that's too bad. What happened?

🕽 **Annabeth Sweet** Well, there's a snowstorm right now, so the flight has been delayed by at least twelve hours.

🕽 **Kathy Sanchez** I see. That means you'll probably arrive around 1:00 A.M.

🕽 **Annabeth Sweet** Yes, I won't be able to attend the meeting. Can we delay it by a day?

🕽 **Kathy Sanchez** I'm sure that won't be a problem. I'll also book a car to pick you up at the airport.

🕽 **Annabeth Sweet** That would be great. Can you recommend a hotel, too? I was planning to fly to L.A. after our meeting, but I'll have to spend the night in New York.

🕽 **Kathy Sanchez** Yes, of course. There's a hotel just down the street from our building. How about if I book a room for you and have the driver take you there?

🕽 **Annabeth Sweet** I would appreciate that. Thank you so much, Kathy!

Pop-up Questions

1 What delayed Ms. Sweet's flight?
2 What does Ms. Sweet ask about the meeting?
3 Where was Ms. Sweet planning to fly to?
4 Where will the driver take Ms. Sweet?

B **Problem Solving ::** Kathy Sanchez gets a call from Annabeth Sweet informing her that the driver she hired never arrived. Find a partner and choose the roles of Kathy Sanchez and Annabeth Sweet. Then, role-play to discuss a possible solution. Use the information from the telephone conversation in A if necessary.

 **Useful Expressions**

A **Let's learn some expressions to use in business.**

When explaining a cancelation	Responding with sympathy
I won't be able to attend the meeting.	Oh, that's too bad.
He can't make it to the airport in time.	I'm sorry to hear that.
They decided not to offer that seminar.	That's unfortunate.
The flight has been canceled.	I can't believe that happened.
When expressing gratitude	**When expressing gratitude for someone else**
I would appreciate that.	Ms. Sweet is very grateful for your help.
I'm so glad you were able to help.	The company appreciates your hard work.
I'm impressed that you solved the problem.	The CEO said you did a great job.

B **Fill in the blanks with the correct answers from the box. Then, practice the conversation with a partner.** 🔊 03-5

I would appreciate that	my flight has been canceled
I won't be able to attend the meeting	I'm sorry to hear that

A Hi, Ms. Parker. This is Jenny Wilson calling.

B Hi, Ms. Wilson. Is there something I can help you with?

A Yes, [1] _____.

B Oh, no. What happened?

A There's a huge snowstorm right now. [2] _____ tomorrow morning.

B [3] _____.

A I think I can get on another flight tomorrow though.

B Okay. In that case, I will pick you up at the airport myself.

A [4] _____.

B It will be no trouble. Just let me know your new arrival time.

Extra Practice

Role-play with your partner. One person mentions a flight was delayed. The other person offers a solution.

A I just found out my flight has been delayed by 4 hours.

B I'm sorry to hear that. I'll send a driver to pick you up.

A I would appreciate that.

B Sure, just let me know your arrival time.

Situation ③

Kathy Sanchez gets a voicemail message from her boss after his meeting. Read it and see if the results are positive or negative. ◀)) 03-6

You have one new message, sent at 2:30 P.M. on February 8.

Hi, Kathy. This is Dan from Management calling. I heard about the mix-up with the car company last night. I can't believe the company accidentally deleted your booking. I'm so glad you were still awake when Ms. Sweet called you. I'm even more impressed that you drove all the way to the airport to pick her up yourself.

Ms. Sweet is very grateful for your help. She mentioned you several times during our meeting. She'd love to take you to lunch as a way to say thank you the next time she's in town.

I know you were at work early this morning. You must be exhausted after being out so late last night. Take the day off tomorrow and get some rest. You deserve a break. Thanks again, Kathy.

Business English Dos and Don'ts

When you are expressing frustration or anger, there are a few ways to do it professionally. Express your disbelief rather than making overly negative statements.

Dos	Don'ts
○ I can't believe the company deleted your booking. (*disbelief*)	✕ That company is the worst. (*too negative*)
○ I'm surprised the delivery arrived so late. (*disbelief*)	✕ He's just awful at his job. (*too negative*)

Speak calmly and thoughtfully. Focus on possible solutions rather than complaining.

Dos	Don'ts
○ I'm not sure it's possible to meet that deadline. (*calm*)	✕ That deadline is impossible! (*complaining*)
○ I think we should discuss this problem. (*thoughtful*)	✕ There is no way to solve this problem! (*complaining*)

Situation ①

Ⓐ **Jan Temple gets an email from Jonathan Stevens asking her to order some office supplies. Read the email.**

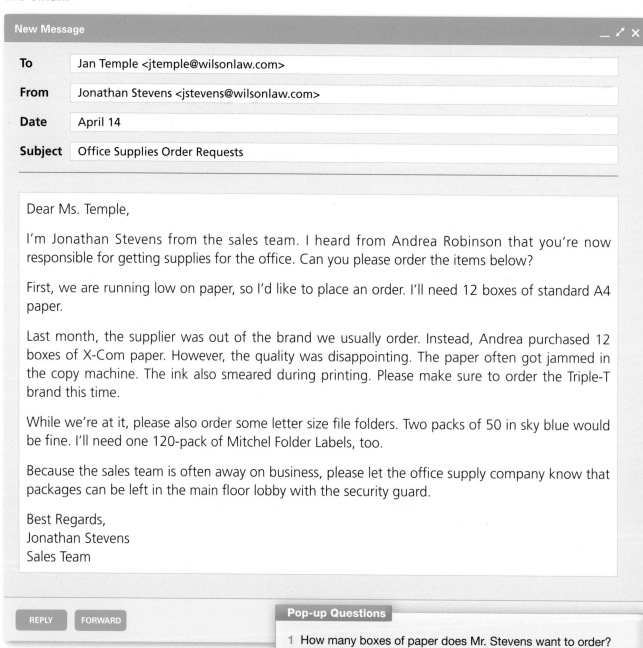

New Message	— ↗ ✕
To	Jan Temple <jtemple@wilsonlaw.com>
From	Jonathan Stevens <jstevens@wilsonlaw.com>
Date	April 14
Subject	Office Supplies Order Requests

Dear Ms. Temple,

I'm Jonathan Stevens from the sales team. I heard from Andrea Robinson that you're now responsible for getting supplies for the office. Can you please order the items below?

First, we are running low on paper, so I'd like to place an order. I'll need 12 boxes of standard A4 paper.

Last month, the supplier was out of the brand we usually order. Instead, Andrea purchased 12 boxes of X-Com paper. However, the quality was disappointing. The paper often got jammed in the copy machine. The ink also smeared during printing. Please make sure to order the Triple-T brand this time.

While we're at it, please also order some letter size file folders. Two packs of 50 in sky blue would be fine. I'll need one 120-pack of Mitchel Folder Labels, too.

Because the sales team is often away on business, please let the office supply company know that packages can be left in the main floor lobby with the security guard.

Best Regards,
Jonathan Stevens
Sales Team

REPLY　FORWARD

Pop-up Questions

1 How many boxes of paper does Mr. Stevens want to order?

2 What happened with the X-Com paper during printing?

3 What other items does Mr. Stevens want to order?

4 Where does Mr. Stevens mention packages can be left?

B Take Notes :: Based on the email in A, complete the order form.

Order Form

Jefferson Office Supplies

Company Name: Wilson Law   *Contact Person:* [1] _____

Address: 34 Parkview Road, 7th floor, Miami, Florida, 33101

Item	Quantity	Unit Price	Total Price
Triple-T [2] _____ (2,000 sheets)	[3] _____	$11.50	$138.00
[4] _____ File Folders (50 sky blue)	2	$6.50	$13.00
Mitchell Folder [5] _____ (120-pack)	[6] _____	$5.99	$5.99

Background Knowledge

A Read and learn about how to order office supplies.

Office supplies are important items that ensure an office runs smoothly. They may include common stationery items, such as pens, paper, and notepads. They may also include items used with electronic equipment, like ink cartridges or toner.

Before ordering office supplies, take an inventory of the supplies currently in the office. Make sure to ask your coworkers what supplies they need. Make a list of all the items you'll need. If one employee usually orders the supplies, give your list to that person.

If you are responsible for ordering supplies, there are a few ways to do that. First, you can call a supplier and place your order over the phone. You might also be able to place an order by email. However, most orders are now placed online. Go to the supply company website. Add items to your cart. Then, pay for the items. Your order will usually be shipped within a few days.

Pop-up Questions

1 What should you do before ordering office supplies?

2 How are most orders placed these days?

B Listen to the conversation and answer the questions. 🔊 04-1

1 **What does Walter need to order?**

a. ink and paper   b. boxes and paper   c. notepads and ink

2 **Who is going to order the office supplies?**

a. Walter   b. Lin   c. Michelle

3 **How will the order be placed?**

a. by email   b. by phone   c. online

Vocabulary

A Look at the pictures and learn some words about office supplies.

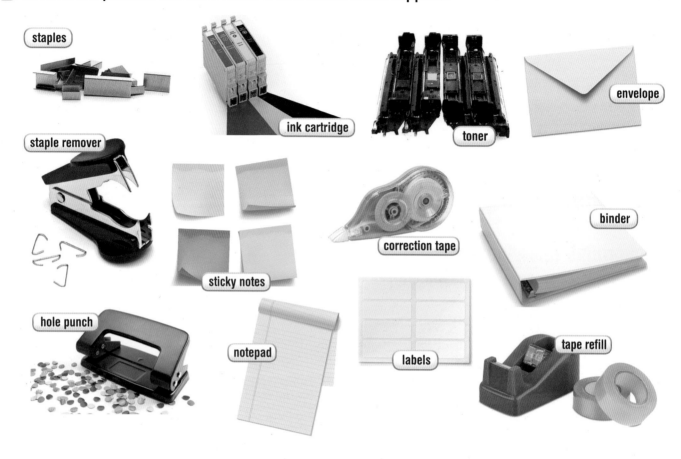

B Complete the sentences with the words in the box.

envelope	notepad	toner	binder
staples	correction tape	staple remover	ink cartridge

1 A stapler is being filled with _____.

2 Put the forms into the _____ and mail it.

3 The assistant wrote the message on a _____.

4 He uses _____ to fix a mistake on the form.

5 You can't copy it now because we're out of _____.

6 He uses the _____ to pull out the staples.

7 I placed all the documents into that _____.

8 Can you order a black _____ for the printer?

Speak Up

Practice the conversation with your partner by using the information on each order form. 🔊 04-2

(Example)

Item	Description	Quantity		Unit Price	Total
Envelopes	Letter Size (100 pack)	˄˅ 4	packs	$5.50	$22.00
Labels	Small (200 pack)	˄˅ 1	pack	$7.99	$7.99
Tape Refills	Clear Stick Tape (3 pack)	˄˅ 5	boxes	$4.99	$24.95
			Delivery ˄˅ Standard		$3.50
			Total		$58.44

Orders will be shipped 1-2 days after payment.

Confirm Order

A It looks like we're out of envelopes.

B I'm placing an order for more right now.

A Thanks. We need 4 packs.

B Let's also order some labels. They're only $7.99 per pack.
   We should get some tape refills, too.

A What's does the total come to?

B It's $58.44 with the delivery fee.

A When will they ship the order?

B The site says they will ship it 1-2 days after payment.

A Is that standard or rush delivery?

B I requested standard.

! Tips for Success

Make a note of the expected delivery date. Some websites offer rush delivery if you need your order quickly.

(Order Form 1)

Item	Description	Quantity	Unit Price	Total
Ink	Ace Tri-Color Ink Cartridges	3 boxes	$40.50	$121.50
Binders	Y-Brand Plastic Binders (3 pack)	10 packs	$4.50	$45.00
Correction Tape	Ink Gone Brand	8 packs	$4.99	$39.92
Delivery Request: Rush			**Delivery**	**$8.50**
Your order will be shipped overnight.			**Total**	**$214.92**

(Order Form 2)

Item	Description	Quantity	Unit Price	Total
Toner	Z-Brand Printer Toner (4 colors)	4 boxes	$89.00	$356.00
Sticky Notes	Stick-Em Sticky Notes (500 pack)	10 packs	$3.50	$35.00
Paper	Plus-M Paper (B5 size)	3 boxes	$8.99	$26.97
Delivery Request: Standard			**Delivery**	**$5.00**
Your order will be shipped tomorrow.			**Total**	**$422.97**

A Let's learn about the present continuous tense.

Present	Future
an action that is happening right now in the present	an action that will happen in the future (+ next week, tomorrow, later...)
Just a moment. I **am looking** for the files. Mr. Jeffrey **is using** the computer in the break room now. I **am walking** to the bank. I'll be there in five minutes.	We **are expecting** a new shipment next week. They **are going** on a long vacation this summer. Linda **is presenting** her report to the CEO tomorrow.

B Complete the following sentences by using the present continuous tense forms of the verbs in the parentheses.

1 I _____ someone to pick up the box right now. (*send*)

2 He _____ to the conference in France next month. (*go*)

3 Please wait a minute. Joe _____ the warehouse about the delay. (*call*)

4 The employees _____ a retirement party for Mr. Park next Friday. (*have*)

5 These days, we _____ on a new logo for the company. (*work*)

6 The company _____ another office in Detroit next year. (*open*)

7 Thomas and Sally _____ in Toronto today and tomorrow. (*stay*)

8 The team _____ an important meeting at 3:00 P.M. tomorrow. (*have*)

🔊 Know-how *at* Work   **How to Manage a Delay**

Delays can inevitably happen. Sometimes a product is sold out. Other times, there is a problem with the shipping company. The company will often contact you to discuss a possible solution.

1 If most of the items are in stock, you can request that those items be sent in advance. The remaining items can be shipped at a later date.

2 If you need an item urgently, you can try a different brand. Ask the company about similar brands. Choose one in a similar price range.

3 Ask the company when the order will be shipped. If some items will be shipped at a later date, get the expected shipping date.

4 Ask for the name and the contact information of the employee who called you. You may need to call that person if there's another problem with the order.

Situation ②

A Jan Temple gets a phone call from Tina Baxter from Jefferson Office Supplies, Inc. Read the telephone conversation. 🔊 04-3

Tina Baxter Hi, Ms. Temple. This is Tina Baxter from Jefferson Office Supplies, Inc.

Jan Temple Hi, Ms. Baxter. How can I help you?

Tina Baxter I just received your order form. Unfortunately, Triple-T A4 paper is currently sold out. We're expecting a new shipment next week.

Jan Temple Oh, I see. It must be a popular item.

Tina Baxter It's one of our bestsellers. Would you like me to send you the rest of your order first?

Jan Temple Well, we're really low on paper. Is it possible to send one box of another brand first?

Tina Baxter Sure. Which brand would you like?

Jan Temple Anything other than the X-Com brand.

Tina Baxter Okay, I will ship your order tomorrow with one box of RX Copy paper. I'll send the remaining eleven boxes of Triple-T A4 paper on April 15.

Jan Temple Great. Thank you.

Tina Baxter Sure. And sorry for the inconvenience!

Pop-up Questions

1 Why is Triple-T A4 paper sold out?

2 What does Ms. Temple ask Ms. Baxter to send first?

3 What brand does Ms. Temple NOT want?

4 When will the rest of the paper be shipped?

B **Problem Solving ::** Jan Temple gets a call from Tina Baxter explaining that the remaining eleven boxes of Triple-T A4 paper are delayed. Find a partner and choose the roles of Jan Temple and Tina Baxter. Then, role-play to discuss a possible solution. Use the information from the telephone conversation in A if necessary.

Useful Expressions

A Let's learn some expressions to use in business.

When suggesting someone do something	When suggesting you will do something
Would you like to order a different brand?	Would you like me to send the rest of your order first?
How about sharing a taxi to the airport?	How about if I ask them to rush the delivery?
I think you should choose standard delivery.	Let me contact the manager of the company.
When you are offering assistance	When you are asking for assistance
How can I help you?	Can you assist me?
What can I help you with?	Could you help me?
Is there something I can help you with?	Would you mind helping me?

B Fill in the blanks with the correct answers from the box. Then, practice the conversation with a partner. ◀))04-4

Let me check your account	Would you like me to rush the delivery
Would you like to order a different brand	How can I help you

A Hello. This is Jim from Janford Accountants.

B Hi, Jim. [1] _____?

A I placed an order last week. It was supposed to arrive yesterday, but it never did.

B [2] _____. Oh, it seems the toner you ordered is out of stock.

A I see. When do you expect a new shipment?

B Not until next week. [3] _____?

A Sure, that would be great.

B How about the Clear Color brand? It's the same price as the one you ordered.

A I'll try it. One box should be good.

B [4] _____?

A Yes, thank you.

Extra Practice

Role-play with your partner. One person mentions some items are out of stock. The other person agrees to order a different brand instead.

A It seems the ink you ordered is out of stock. Would you like to order a different brand?

B Sure, that would be great.

A How about the Ace brand?

B I'll try it. Two boxes should be good.

Situation 3

Jan Temple gets an instant message from Jonathan Stevens on April 16, which is the day after the remaining eleven boxes of paper are scheduled to be sent. Read it and see if the results are positive or negative.

Jonathan Stevens

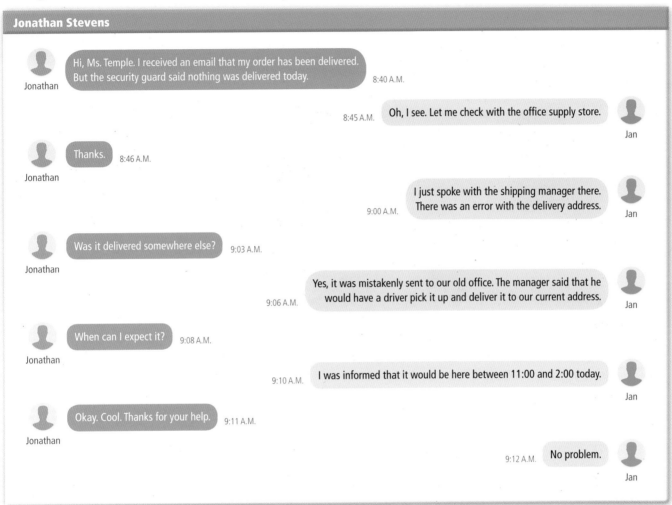

Jonathan: Hi, Ms. Temple. I received an email that my order has been delivered. But the security guard said nothing was delivered today. 8:40 A.M.

8:45 A.M. **Jan:** Oh, I see. Let me check with the office supply store.

Jonathan: Thanks. 8:46 A.M.

9:00 A.M. **Jan:** I just spoke with the shipping manager there. There was an error with the delivery address.

Jonathan: Was it delivered somewhere else? 9:03 A.M.

9:06 A.M. **Jan:** Yes, it was mistakenly sent to our old office. The manager said that he would have a driver pick it up and deliver it to our current address.

Jonathan: When can I expect it? 9:08 A.M.

9:10 A.M. **Jan:** I was informed that it would be here between 11:00 and 2:00 today.

Jonathan: Okay. Cool. Thanks for your help. 9:11 A.M.

9:12 A.M. **Jan:** No problem.

Business English Dos and Don'ts

When you are solving a problem with your coworker, there are some important things to remember. Be as specific as possible about times, dates, and the course of action you will take.

Dos	Don'ts
○ Let me check with the Shipping Department. (*specific*)	✕ I'll ask the new guy. (*vague*)
○ It'll be there between 11:00 and 12:00 today. (*specific*)	✕ It might arrive sometime today but maybe not. (*vague*)

Choose words and phrases that are neutral rather than negative or emotional.

Dos	Don'ts
○ There was an error with the shipping address. (*neutral*)	✕ Ted wrote the wrong shipping address again! (*negative*)
○ It was mistakenly sent to our old office. (*neutral*)	✕ I can't believe they sent it to our old office! (*emotional*)

Applying for a Training Session

Situation ❶

A **Ellen Church is discussing some training programs with her coworker, Stephanie Paige. Read the conversation.** 🔊 05-1

S   Hi, Ellen. Did you see the training program list corporate emailed this morning for the fall training session?

E   I looked at it briefly. Are you going to attend any of the workshops?

S   I'm thinking of applying for the social media management workshop.

E   That's a good idea. Social media is so important for marketing these days.

S   Will you apply for anything this year?

E   I want to apply for the leadership training course. I was promoted to team leader a couple of months ago, but I'd like to improve my skills as a leader.

S   That sounds great. When are the leadership classes?

E   They're being held in auditorium 1 at our corporate headquarters in Springfield from 10:00 A.M. to 4:00 P.M. on October 20.

S   Mine will be in auditorium 2 from 10:00 A.M. to 3:00 P.M. on the same day. We should carpool.

E   Sure, I'd love that.

S   Great. Just make sure to submit your application by next Friday.

E   Oh, actually, mine is due next Thursday. Thanks for the reminder though.

Pop-up Questions

1   When did the workers receive the email?

2   What will Ms. Paige apply for?

3   What happened to Ms. Church a couple of months ago?

4   How does Ms. Paige suggest she and Ms. Church get to the office?

B Take Notes :: Based on the conversation in A, complete the schedule with information about the training programs.

	Topic	Location	Date	Time	Deadline for Applications
Ellen Church	1	2	3	4	5
Stephanie Paige	6	7	8	9	10

Background Knowledge

A Read and learn about types of employee training programs.

Education and training are important parts of professional development. When new employees are hired, they often go through an orientation period. They learn about the company and how to do their jobs properly.

However, employees who have been working at a company for longer might also receive training. Some employees need technical skills training. They can learn more about coding, data analysis, or social media management. Other employees might need product and service training. These classes help employees learn more about the products and services a company offers. Employees who deal with customers should take soft skills training. They can learn to communicate and solve problems effectively.

Team leaders and managers should take a variety of training courses. They must know how to lead others, how to manage day-to-day duties, and how to solve problems. Non-managers can take management courses as well. This helps them prepare for the future and get promotions. Many companies offer ethics training to all their employees. Ethics training helps employees follow laws, understand company codes, and make moral choices.

Pop-up Questions

1 What type of training do new employees receive?
2 Which type of training teaches data analysis?

B Listen to the conversation and answer the questions. 🔊 05-2

1 **When will Jenny go to the head office?**
   a. Wednesday   b. Thursday   c. next year

2 **What training program will Jenny take?**
   a. social media management   b. technical skills training   c. product and service training

3 **What will the company do next year?**
   a. train some workers   b. use social media   c. launch some products

Vocabulary

A Look at the pictures and learn some topics related to training programs.

diversity

time management

leadership

problem-solving

presentation

social media

teamwork

conflict resolution

B Complete the sentences with the words in the box.

teamwork	social media	conflict resolution	problem-solving
leadership	diversity	presentation	time management

1 The company is committed to _____. It promises to hire people of all genders, races, religions, and nationalities.

2 The _____ class taught Mr. Lim how to resolve arguments. It showed him how to prevent conflicts, too.

3 Our company is popular with young people because we advertise our products on many _____ websites.

4 I would love to watch his _____ on coding. I need to improve my coding skills if I want to get a promotion.

5 The members of the Marketing Department worked well together on the project. The manager praised them for their _____.

6 Robert attended the workshop on becoming a leader last month. I think it really improved his _____ skills.

7 When I have a difficult problem, I ask my manager, Wendy, for help. She has excellent _____ skills.

8 How are you at _____? If you're hired, you'll have to manage many projects at once. You'll also have to work quickly.

Speak Up

Practice the conversation with your partner by using the information on the training program schedule. 05-3

Spring Training Program Schedule

*all classes will be held at our corporate headquarters in Ottawa
*free parking will be available for employees traveling from out of town

Program	Day	Date	Time	Location	Courses
Management Training	Monday	April 2	10:00 A.M. – 2:00 P.M.	Conference Room 5, second floor	Conflict Resolution / Leadership Skills / Project Management
Technical Skills Training	Monday	April 2	10:30 A.M. – 3:50 P.M.	Auditorium 1, first floor	Data Analysis / Social Media Management / Coding
Product and Service Training	Tuesday	April 3	11:00 A.M. – 3:00 P.M.	Auditorium 1, first floor	New Products / New Services
Soft Skills Training	Tuesday	April 3	10:30 A.M. – 3:40 P.M.	Auditorium 2, first floor	Communication Skills / Time Management / Teamwork
Ethics Training	Friday	April 5	9:30 A.M. – 5:30 P.M.	Conference Room 4, third floor	Ethical Conduct / Diversity / Customer Privacy

A Hi. Did you see the schedule for the spring training program?

B Yes, I'm going to take technical skills training.

A What sort of classes are in that program?

B There are a few, but I'm looking forward to the coding class.

A Oh, I see. I'm going to take product and service training.

B When are your classes?

A On Tuesday, April 3, from 11:00 A.M. to 3:00 P.M.

B Mine are in Auditorium 1 on April 2.

A We should probably arrive early just in case we get lost.

B That's a good idea!

Tips for Success

When planning to attend a training session, make sure to note the time and the location. Arrive early in case you have trouble finding your room.

A Let's learn about the modal verb *should*.

Positive / Negative	Interrogative
Use **should (not) + verb (base form of the infinitive)** to offer advice, to show an appropriate course of action, and to make a suggestion.	Use **should + pronoun + verb (base form of the infinitive)** in a question to ask for advice or an appropriate course of action.
You **should talk** to him about the problem. They **should not use** the emergency exit. We **should carpool** to the conference	**Should I apply** for the marketing position? **Should we submit** the documents to Mr. Lee? **Should our team hire** a new employee?

B Complete the sentences with the words in the box. Add *should* to the sentences.

apply	hire	meet	carpool	email	request	reserve	have

1 _____ we _____ him in the conference room?

2 You _____ a leave of absence.

3 Jenny _____ her itinerary to me by Friday.

4 _____ I _____ for the management position?

5 He will retire soon. You _____ a new employee.

6 The department _____ a meeting about the complaint.

7 _____ I _____ the theater for our presentation?

8 They _____ to work. It's better for the environment.

📶 Know-how *at* Work   **How to Attend a Training Session**

Training sessions can happen at various times throughout the year. If you wish to attend one, there are a few steps to follow to ensure your experience is pleasant.

1 Select the program you'd like to apply for. Fill out an application form and submit it on time. If you submit it late, you might not be able to attend.

2 Take note of the time and the date of the session. If it occurs during working hours, you must contact your manager. Ask if you can miss work that day to attend the session.

3 If the session is at an unfamiliar location, try to arrive early. Ask a receptionist or security guard for directions to your assigned room.

4 Some training sessions run all day. Inquire in advance if it will be a catered event. If not, plan to bring a lunch and beverages. You can go to a nearby restaurant or café for lunch as well.

Situation 2

A Ellen Church sends an instant message to her manager to ask if it's okay to attend a training session during working hours. Read the message chain.

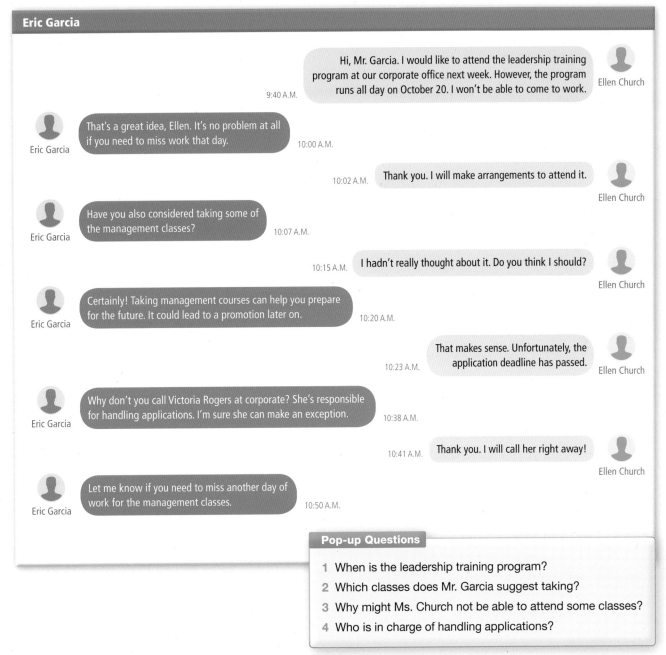

Eric Garcia

Hi, Mr. Garcia. I would like to attend the leadership training program at our corporate office next week. However, the program runs all day on October 20. I won't be able to come to work.
9:40 A.M. — Ellen Church

That's a great idea, Ellen. It's no problem at all if you need to miss work that day.
Eric Garcia — *10:00 A.M.*

Thank you. I will make arrangements to attend it.
10:02 A.M. — Ellen Church

Have you also considered taking some of the management classes?
Eric Garcia — *10:07 A.M.*

I hadn't really thought about it. Do you think I should?
10:15 A.M. — Ellen Church

Certainly! Taking management courses can help you prepare for the future. It could lead to a promotion later on.
Eric Garcia — *10:20 A.M.*

That makes sense. Unfortunately, the application deadline has passed.
10:23 A.M. — Ellen Church

Why don't you call Victoria Rogers at corporate? She's responsible for handling applications. I'm sure she can make an exception.
Eric Garcia — *10:38 A.M.*

Thank you. I will call her right away!
10:41 A.M. — Ellen Church

Let me know if you need to miss another day of work for the management classes.
Eric Garcia — *10:50 A.M.*

Pop-up Questions

1 When is the leadership training program?

2 Which classes does Mr. Garcia suggest taking?

3 Why might Ms. Church not be able to attend some classes?

4 Who is in charge of handling applications?

B **Problem Solving ::** Ellen Church must call Victoria Rogers and ask if she can still apply for the program her manager recommended. Find a partner and choose the roles of Ellen Church and Victoria Rogers. Then, role-play to discuss a possible solution. Use the information from the instant message chain in A if necessary.

Useful Expressions

A Let's learn some expressions to use in business.

When promising to do something	When asking to be informed
I will call her right away.	Let me know if you need time off.
I will email you as soon as possible.	Fill me in when you can.
I will contact you shortly with an answer.	Get back to me about it.
I will start on the proposal straight away.	Keep me posted.
When providing assurance	**When providing reassurance**
Certainly!	It's no problem at all.
Of course, I will.	It's perfectly fine. Don't worry.
I can definitely do that.	It won't be any trouble at all.

B Fill in the blanks with the correct answers from the box. Then, practice the conversation with a partner. 🔊 05-4

I will ask her right away	It won't be any trouble
Fill me in when you can	Certainly

A Hello, Mr. Kang. I'm thinking of attending the marketing training course.

B That's a great idea. I think you'll enjoy it.

A Yes, but we have our monthly marketing meeting that day. Can I miss it?

B ¹ _____. You can ask Anna to fill in for you.

A Good idea. ² _____.

B Great. Have you considered also attending the social media management class?

A I have, but I would have to miss another day of work. Are you sure that's okay?

B ³ _____ at all. Don't worry.

A Okay, I will apply for that one, too.

B Good. ⁴ _____.

A Will do! Thanks, Mr. Kang.

Extra Practice

Role-play with your partner. One person asks about attending a training session. The other person suggests an additional class.

A I'd like to attend the management training program. Can I miss work that day?

B Certainly! Have you considered taking ethics training, too?

A Yes, but I'd have to miss another day of work. Is that okay?

B It's perfectly fine. Don't worry!

Situation ③

Ellen Church sends an email to Victoria Rogers to provide feedback about the fall training session. Read it and see if the results are positive or negative.

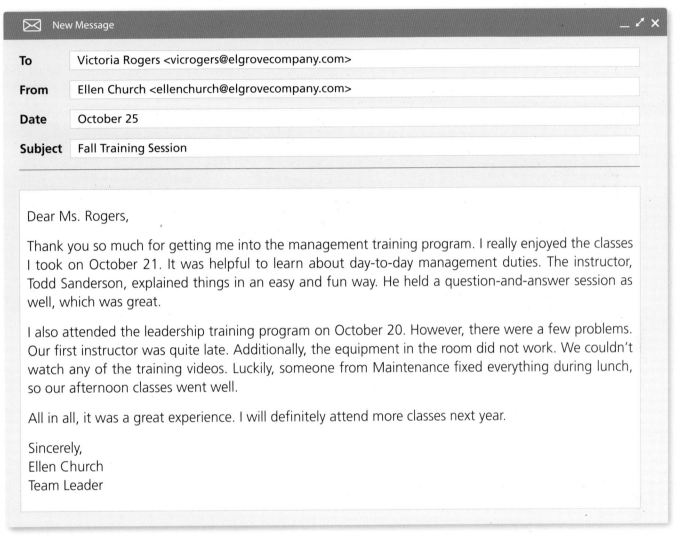

> ✉ New Message   ─ ↗ ✕
>
> **To**   Victoria Rogers <vicrogers@elgrovecompany.com>
>
> **From**   Ellen Church <ellenchurch@elgrovecompany.com>
>
> **Date**   October 25
>
> **Subject**   Fall Training Session
>
> ---
>
> Dear Ms. Rogers,
>
> Thank you so much for getting me into the management training program. I really enjoyed the classes I took on October 21. It was helpful to learn about day-to-day management duties. The instructor, Todd Sanderson, explained things in an easy and fun way. He held a question-and-answer session as well, which was great.
>
> I also attended the leadership training program on October 20. However, there were a few problems. Our first instructor was quite late. Additionally, the equipment in the room did not work. We couldn't watch any of the training videos. Luckily, someone from Maintenance fixed everything during lunch, so our afternoon classes went well.
>
> All in all, it was a great experience. I will definitely attend more classes next year.
>
> Sincerely,
> Ellen Church
> Team Leader

Business English Dos and Don'ts

When you are providing written feedback about a company event, there are a few things to remember. Explain problems that occurred in a neutral way. Don't use dramatic phrases.

Dos	**Don'ts**
○ Our first instructor was quite late. (*neutral*)	✗ We waited around for hours! (*dramatic*)
○ The equipment in the room didn't work. (*neutral*)	✗ As usual, none of the equipment worked. (*dramatic*)

Summarize your feedback at the end of your message. Speak generally about the whole event.

Dos	**Don'ts**
○ All in all, it was a great experience. (*summary*)	✗ I enjoyed the refreshments. (*too specific*)
○ On the whole, we learned a lot. (*summary*)	✗ I couldn't find my seat in the banquet hall. (*too specific*)

Situation ❶

A **Jeffrey Black is discussing his summer vacation plans with his coworker, Rebecca Lafleur. Read the conversation.** 📢 06-1

R Is that a brochure for Hawaii? Are you taking a trip?

J Yes, my family and I are planning to go there for two weeks next month.

R That's amazing. I'm so envious. I've always wanted to go to Hawaii.

J Are you taking a vacation this summer?

R I'm not going anywhere this year. Last year, I went to Paris for a week. It was wonderful but quite expensive. I'd prefer to save my money this year.

J I understand. The flights can be so pricey.

R So when are you leaving?

J I'll be gone from June 15 to 26.

R Oh, you know the Operations Department has an orientation session for new hires on the 18th, right? Aren't you going to lead the warehouse tour?

J Are you sure? I was told that was happening next week.

R Maybe you missed the email. It was rescheduled.

J Hmm... That's a problem. I'll speak to the manager about it.

Pop-up Questions

1 Where is Mr. Black going for his vacation?

2 Where did Ms. Lafleur go last year?

3 What does the Operations Department have on June 18?

4 What was Mr. Black going to lead?

B Take Notes :: Based on the conversation in A, complete the time-off request form.

Employee Time-off Request Form

Today's Date: May 13

Employee Department: ¹_____

Employee Name: ²_____

Time-off Request: ³*(Days / Hours)*

Beginning on: ⁴_____   *Ending on:* ⁵_____

Reason for Request: ⁶*(Vacation / Funeral / Jury Duty / Medical Leave / To Vote / Others)*

Background Knowledge

A Read and learn about asking for time off work.

There are many reasons why employees might need to take time off from work. Taking a vacation, attending a funeral, and doing jury duty are all reasons to take a few days off. A leave of absence, such as for maternity or medical leave, is a longer period of time off. When asking for time off, there are a few things to remember.

Make sure your information is accurate when you fill out a time-off request form. Write down the dates you will be absent. Add your full name and department. You should also add the date you are submitting the request form. You should note the reason you will be away, too.

Try to submit your time-off request form as early as possible. In the event of a vacation or maternity leave, submit your request a few weeks or months in advance. This will help your company prepare for your absence. However, sometimes things such as a death in the family happen unexpectedly. Contact your manager as soon as possible. Let your company know what happened and how long you'll be away.

Pop-up Questions

1 What should you note on your time-off request form?

2 Why should you submit your request a few weeks or months in advance?

B Listen to the voicemail and answer the questions. ◀)) 06-2

1 **Why does Margaret request time off?**

   a. to go on vacation   b. to take medical leave   c. to attend a funeral

2 **When will Margaret's time off begin?**

   a. today   b. tomorrow   c. Wednesday

3 **How can Mr. West contact Margaret?**

   a. by phone   b. by email   c. through Catherine

Vocabulary

A Look at the pictures and learn some reasons for taking time off work.

 vacation
 bereavement
 jury duty
 medical

 voting
 maternity/paternity
 military
 wedding

B Complete the sentences with the words in the box.

medical	vacation	paternity	voting
wedding	bereavement	jury duty	military

1 Miranda had an accident while she was skiing in Switzerland. She broke her leg and requested
_____ since she'll be unable to get around for at least six weeks.

2 My brother is getting married in Jamaica next year. I'm planning to ask for a week off to attend
the _____ next March.

3 Mrs. Anderson's husband passed away last week. She requested a three-month _____
leave, so we're going to hire a temporary replacement for that time.

4 Joseph's wife is going to give birth to twins soon. He'll be taking _____ leave
starting next month. However, he's going to work from home part time.

5 The presidential election is today, so we don't have to work this afternoon. I know who I'm
_____ for.

6 Beth is flying to Spain for a three-week _____. I've always wanted to go to Spain. I
heard the food there is amazing!

7 I just found out Michael will be on _____ leave for a year. I didn't know he joined
the National Guard.

8 Sammy got a letter telling her to report for _____. Apparently, the trial will begin
next month, but I'm not sure how long she'll be gone.

Speak Up

Practice the conversation with your partner by using the information in each time-off request form.

🔊 06-3

Example

Today's Date: January 6

Employee Department: Marketing

Employee Name: Carlo Alberto

Time-off Request: ☑ Days ☐ Hours

Beginning on: January 7

Ending on: January 10

Reason for Request: attending my grandfather's funeral

Example

Today's Date: January 6

Employee Department: Marketing

Employee Name: Carlo Alberto

Time-off Request: ☑ Days ☐ Hours

Beginning on: January 7

Ending on: January 10

Reason for Request: attending my grandfather's funeral

Form 2

Today's Date: February 7

Employee Department: Sales

Employee Name: Constance Bell

Time-off Request: ☑ Days ☐ Hours

Beginning on: April 1

Ending on: September 30

Reason for Request: taking maternity leave

Form 3

Today's Date: August 10

Employee Department: Operations

Employee Name: Farid Azeez

Time-off Request: ☐ Days ☑ Hours

Beginning on: August 11 at 1:00 P.M.

Ending on: August 11 at 4:00 P.M.

Reason for Request: attending my son's graduation

A Hello, Ms. Samuels. Here is my time-off request form.

B Thank you, Carlo. Can you add today's date, January 6?

A Sure. Here you are.

B Thanks. So you'll be away from January 7?

A Yes, that's right.

B Oh, you forgot to write down the reason.

A I'll be attending my grandfather's funeral.

B Oh, I see. How long will you be gone?

A Until January 10. Should I ask someone to fill in for me?

B No, I think the Marketing Department can manage just fine.

! Tips for Success

When filling out a time-off request form, write down the dates you will be gone as well as the date you completed the form.

A **Let's learn about the future continuous tense.**

Positive / Negative	Interrogative
Use **will be + verb + -ing** to refer to an unfinished action or an action that will continue at a later time.	Use **will + pronoun + be + verb + -ing** to ask about an unfinished action or an action that will continue at a later time.
I **will be teaching** free classes online next month. They **will be having** lunch when you arrive. Ms. Pham **will be working** from home from now on.	**Will you be sharing** your idea tomorrow? **Will they be using** the same computer? **Will we be collecting** donations for the charity?

B **Complete the sentences by using the future continuous tense forms of the verbs in parentheses.**

1 The company _____ a survey that day. (*conduct*)

2 _____ at the conference this spring? (*you + speak*)

3 He _____ in Mexico during the holiday. (*travel*)

4 I _____ my invention at the technology fair again this year. (*show*)

5 _____ our office at all this winter? (*they + visit*)

6 _____ an office for the rest of the year? (*we + share*)

7 The owner _____ the first floor for the next few months. (*renovate*)

8 _____ from home during your maternity leave? (*you + work*)

Know-how *at* **Work**   **How to Prepare for an Absence**

Most employees must apply for time off at some point during their careers. However, being absent could disrupt your coworkers and leave them with extra work. There are a few ways to prepare for your absence.

1 If you're going to be away for a short time, try to finish your work in advance. Make sure you've met your deadlines. Otherwise, your coworkers may need to finish your work for you.

2 Some absences can last several months. In that case, you might need a temporary replacement. You might be asked to hire someone. Ask your Human Resources Department for help.

3 If a replacement has been hired, he or she might need training. You should take the time to show him or her how to do your job well.

4 Sometimes your coworkers will take some of your workload. Before you leave, communicate with them. Answer any questions they might have about your job duties.

Situation ②

A Jeffrey Black sends an instant message to his manager to ask if it's okay to take a vacation. Read the message chain.

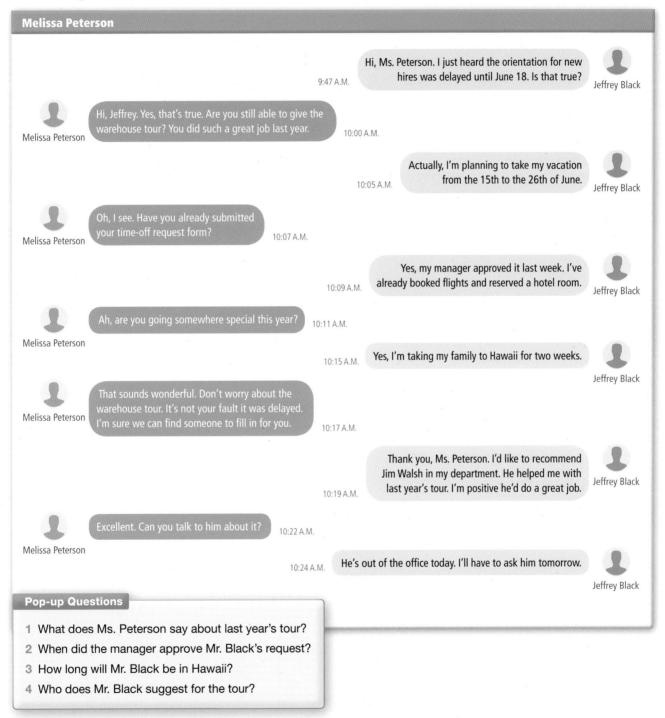

Melissa Peterson

> Hi, Ms. Peterson. I just heard the orientation for new hires was delayed until June 18. Is that true?
> 9:47 A.M. — Jeffrey Black

> Hi, Jeffrey. Yes, that's true. Are you still able to give the warehouse tour? You did such a great job last year.
> Melissa Peterson — 10:00 A.M.

> Actually, I'm planning to take my vacation from the 15th to the 26th of June.
> 10:05 A.M. — Jeffrey Black

> Oh, I see. Have you already submitted your time-off request form?
> Melissa Peterson — 10:07 A.M.

> Yes, my manager approved it last week. I've already booked flights and reserved a hotel room.
> 10:09 A.M. — Jeffrey Black

> Ah, are you going somewhere special this year?
> Melissa Peterson — 10:11 A.M.

> Yes, I'm taking my family to Hawaii for two weeks.
> 10:15 A.M. — Jeffrey Black

> That sounds wonderful. Don't worry about the warehouse tour. It's not your fault it was delayed. I'm sure we can find someone to fill in for you.
> Melissa Peterson — 10:17 A.M.

> Thank you, Ms. Peterson. I'd like to recommend Jim Walsh in my department. He helped me with last year's tour. I'm positive he'd do a great job.
> 10:19 A.M. — Jeffrey Black

> Excellent. Can you talk to him about it?
> Melissa Peterson — 10:22 A.M.

> He's out of the office today. I'll have to ask him tomorrow.
> 10:24 A.M. — Jeffrey Black

Pop-up Questions

1 What does Ms. Peterson say about last year's tour?
2 When did the manager approve Mr. Black's request?
3 How long will Mr. Black be in Hawaii?
4 Who does Mr. Black suggest for the tour?

B **Problem Solving :: Jim Walsh is unable to give the warehouse tour. Jeffrey Black must ask another colleague if he or she can complete the task. Find a partner and choose the roles of Jeffrey Black and his colleague. Then, role-play to discuss a possible solution. Use the information from the instant message chain in A if necessary.**

A **Let's learn some expressions to use in business.**

When relaying prior knowledge or instructions	When expressing the necessity of an action
I just heard the orientation was delayed.	I'll have to ask him tomorrow.
I was told that was happening next week.	I'll need to see the documents again.
He informed me that the flight was canceled.	I'm going to need your signature.
The CEO let me know about the change.	I must speak with the manager today.
When expressing certainty	**When expressing approval**
I'm positive he'd do a great job.	Excellent.
I'm certain she deserves the promotion.	Wonderful.
I'm sure he won't mind the change.	That's great.

B **Fill in the blanks with the correct answers from the box. Then, practice the conversation with a partner.** 📢 06-4

Wonderful	I'm going to need your signature
My doctor told me I need to have surgery	I'm positive she'd do a great job

A Hi, Ms. Lynd. I know it's short notice, but I need to take medical leave.

B I'm sorry to hear that. How long do you need?

A About three weeks. ¹_____.

B I hope it's not serious. Is there someone who can fill in for you?

A Well, I was going to suggest Jack Woods.

B Hmm, I'm not sure he's the best candidate. He was only hired last month.

A Right. Do you have anyone else in mind?

B How about Tammy in Sales? ²_____.

A All right. I'll speak to Tammy about it today.

B ³_____. Let me know if there are any problems.

A Oh, one more thing. ⁴_____ on my time-off request.

B Sure. No problem.

Extra Practice

Role-play with your partner. One person needs to take time off. The other person approves the request.

A Hi. I need to take some time off to attend a funeral.

B Of course. Is there someone who can fill in for you?

A I was going to suggest Cole Mills. I'm positive he'd do a great job.

B Excellent. I'll speak with him today.

Situation 3

Jeffrey Black finds the orientation schedule for next month on the bulletin board. Look at it and see if the results are positive or negative.

Orientation Schedule

Time	Event	Description
9:00 – 10:00	Meet and Greet	Roz Campino in Human Resources will greet new hires in Auditorium 2.
10:00 – 12:00	Warehouse Tour	Lisbeth Fry in the Operations Department will conduct the tour of our five warehouses and also give a safety demonstration.
12:00 – 1:00	Catered Lunch	A lunch catered by Wholesome Foods will be served in the office lounge on the first floor.
1:00 – 3:00	Department Specific Training	New hires will split up and head to their respective departments. The following employees will conduct the training: Sale Department – Christina Wells Operations Department – Lisbeth Fry Marketing Department – Xander Sigmont Accounting Department – Pierre McDonald
3:00 – 4:00	Rules and Regulations	New hires will regroup in Auditorium 2 for a presentation on company rules and regulations given by Roz Campino.

Date of Event June 18

Please Note

This schedule is considered final. Time-off request forms for June 18 will not be approved unless there is an emergency. If your time-off request has already been approved, this does not apply to you.

Business English Dos and Don'ts

When you must assert the rules in a written notice, there are a few things to consider. Be formal and firm. Try not to complain, threaten, or use unprofessional words.

Dos
- ○ This schedule is considered final. (*formal*)
- ○ Time-off requests will not be approved. (*firm*)

Don'ts
- ✕ Don't ask me to change the schedule again! (*unprofessional*)
- ✕ Submitting a request will really annoy management. (*complaining*)

Be as concise as possible. Long or vague explanations can confuse employees.

Dos
- ○ It won't be approved unless there is an emergency. (*concise*)
- ○ This does not apply to the Sales Department. (*concise*)

Don'ts
- ✕ It might be approved, but it depends on what type of emergency and how many employees are... (*too long*)
- ✕ A few departments might be exempt. (*vague*)

Situation ①

A Mathew Fernsby gets a phone call from a potential customer. Read the telephone conversation.

 07-1

Bethany Morton Hello. This is Bethany Morton calling.

Mathew Fernsby Hello, Ms. Morton. How can I help you?

Bethany Morton I'm the district manager of twenty fitness clubs in the Greater Toronto Area. I'm interested in selling your company's energy drinks at my clubs.

Mathew Fernsby Oh, I see. I think I should transfer you to the Sales Department.

Bethany Morton I'm sorry. Are you not Bob Peterson, the sales manager?

Mathew Fernsby No, this is the Accounting Department. Hold for a moment, please. I'll see if he's available.

Bethany Morton Okay, thank you.

Mathew Fernsby Ms. Morton, thank you for holding. The sales team is currently out of the office. Can I take a message instead?

Bethany Morton Sure. Can you ask Mr. Peterson to call me back?

Mathew Fernsby No problem. Can I get your phone number and business name?

Bethany Morton It's Universal Fitness, and the number is 905-643-0219.

Mathew Fernsby Okay, great. I will pass the message along to Bob. He'll be in touch soon to discuss supplying your clubs with our energy drinks.

Bethany Morton Thanks. Have a great day.

Pop-up Questions

1 What is Ms. Morton's job?
2 Who was Ms. Morton trying to call?
3 Where is the sales team currently?
4 Why will Mr. Fernsby contact Mr. Peterson?

B **Take Notes** :: Based on the telephone conversation in A, complete the message.

September 26, 2:45 P.M.

To: [1] _____   From: [2] _____ (Tel. 905-643-0219)

Business Name: [3] _____

Message: Bethany Morton is the [4] _____ at Universal Fitness. She manages twenty [5] _____ and wants to sell our [6] _____ there. Please call her back as soon as possible.

Message Taken By: [7] _____ in Accounting

Background Knowledge

A **Read and learn about how to handle customer inquiries over the phone.**

Making sure customer inquiries are handled well is essential for good customer relations. Oftentimes, customers will call to ask questions about products and services. Potential customers will also have inquiries. There are a few things to remember when handling customer inquiries over the phone.

First, greet the customer politely. Introduce yourself and mention the department you work in. Gather the customer's information, such as his or her name, company, and position at the company. Next, find out why the customer is calling. Take notes as the customer explains the inquiry.

If you can, answer the customer's questions. However, if you must pass the inquiry to another department, write down the customer's contact information. Repeat the inquiry and promise to pass it to your coworker as soon as possible. Finally, politely thank the customer for calling.

Pop-up Questions

1 What should you do first when talking to a customer?
2 What should you do last when handling an inquiry?

B **Listen to the conversation and answer the questions.** 🔊 07-2

1 **What does Mr. Black want to sell at his shop?**
   a. T-shirts   b. sweaters   c. pants

2 **Where does Ms. White say she works?**
   a. Human Resources   b. Sales   c. Urban Style

3 **What does Ms. White offer to do?**
   a. call Tim   b. deliver a message   c. send some sweaters

Vocabulary

A **Learn some departments in a company.**

1	Sales and Marketing	builds customer relationships and develops promotional materials in order to sell products
2	Human Resources	hires and trains new employees in addition to managing disputes
3	Accounting	keeps detailed records of incoming and outgoing finances
4	Production and Manufacturing	manufactures products, orders inventory, and fills product orders
5	Purchasing	purchases materials or products needed for the business to operate
6	Administration	oversees employees and implements new company initiatives
7	Information Technology	installs and maintains the computer network in an office
8	Public Relations	develops and maintains a company's image
9	Research and Development	researches and develops new products while also improving existing products
10	Operations	controls production schedules and ensures the company is running smoothly

B **Read the sentences on the left and match them with the correct departments on the right.**

1 You have to give expense receipts to the _____ Department.   •

2 The _____ Department came up with a new TV commercial.   •

3 Please send all résumés to the _____ Department.   •

4 The Internet isn't working. I'll call the _____ Department.   •

5 _____ needs a new manager to oversee the office.   •

6 The _____ Department released a statement about the CEO's unprofessional comment.   •

7 Send the production schedule to the _____ Department for approval.   •

8 _____ will start developing a new product line this year.   •

• a. Human Resources

• b. Operations

• c. Accounting

• d. Administration

• e. Sales and Marketing

• f. Public Relations

• g. Information Technology

• h. Research and Development

Speak Up

Practice the conversation with your partner by using the information in each message. 🔊 07-3

Example

March 14, 9:55 A.M.

To: Greg Wilson

From: Randy Jennings (Tel. 443-213-9987)

Business Name: Sugar King Bakery

Message: Randy Jennings is the owner of the Sugar King Bakery. He is interested in doing some advertising for his bakery. Please call him back as soon as possible.

Message Taken By: Trisha Garcia in Sales

Message 1

June 28, 2:24 P.M.

To: Sammy Weeks

From: May Hong (Tel. 332-124-0098)

Business Name: Weston Jewelry

Message: May Hong is the head manager of Weston Jewelry. She is interested in advertising a sale on our website. Please call her back as soon as possible.

Message Taken By: Alicia Pierce in Operations

Message 2

October 10, 10:05 A.M.

To: Leah Parker

From: Alison Fox (Tel. 222-785-0087)

Business Name: Hampton Veterinary Clinic

Message: Alison Fox is the owner of the Hampton Veterinary Clinic. She is interested in advertising a fundraiser to help stray animals in the city. Please call her back as soon as possible.

Message Taken By: Samantha Wallace in Accounting

Message 3

April 21, 3:31 P.M.

To: Jason White

From: Peter Grimes (Tel. 554-223-1109)

Business Name: Comfort Home and Décor

Message: Peter Grimes is the manager of Comfort Home and Décor. He is interested in advertising a summer sale in the next few months. Please call him back as soon as possible.

Message Taken By: Albert Richards in Human Resources

A Hello. This is Randy Jennings. I'm the owner of the Sugar King Bakery.

B Hi. How can I help you?

A I'm interested in doing some advertising for my bakery.

B I think you need to speak with someone in the Marketing Department.

A Oh, is this not the Marketing Department?

B No, this is Trisha Garcia in Sales. Let me connect you.

A Thank you.

B Thanks for holding. Everyone in the Marketing Department is currently in a meeting.

A Okay. Can you have someone call me back at 443-213-9987?

B Sure. Greg Wilson will call you shortly to discuss advertising.

! Tips for Success

If a customer calls you by mistake, don't hang up. Offer to connect him or her to the correct department.

GRAMMAR

A **Let's learn about gerunds after prepositions.**

verb + preposition + gerund	be verb + adjective + preposition + gerund
We **worried about losing** the client.	I **am interested in applying** for the grant.
He **insists on meeting** you in person.	He **was afraid of losing** his car keys and wallet.
The CEO **believes in treating** his employees well.	She **is sorry for making** a mess in the breakroom.
She **apologized for missing** the meeting.	Tom **is excited about joining** the company.
The employee **complained about losing** his vacation.	The manager **is concerned about raising** salaries.

B **Complete the following sentences by using the infinitives in the parentheses. Change the verbs to the past tense. Use the gerund form of the second infinitive.**

1 Mr. Brown _____ about _____ his job. (*talk* + *quit*)

2 The employees _____ to _____ late on Fridays. (*object* + *work*)

3 The clients _____ unsure about _____ more on advertising. (*be* + *spend*)

4 Cindy _____ interested in _____ for the position. (*be* + *apply*)

5 I _____ for _____ late several times this month. (*apologize* + *be*)

6 The deliveryman _____ about _____ lost again. (*worry* + *get*)

7 The customer _____ sorry for _____ the payment late. (*be* + *send*)

8 Ms. Bell _____ in _____ her employees. (*believe* + *reward*)

Know-how *at* Work   **How to Deliver Customer Inquiries**

Communication between departments is important. Sometimes a customer has questions for someone in another department. You can deliver a detailed message to your coworker.

1 When relaying a customer inquiry, first, introduce yourself. Give your name and department. You can also mention your position.

2 Explain in detail why you called. If you're delivering a message on behalf of a customer, mention why the customer called.

3 Let your coworker know how to proceed. If the customer wants to be contacted, provide the correct phone number. Mention if the situation is urgent.

4 Deliver customer inquiries as soon as possible. If your coworker is out of the office, send a text message or call his or her cell phone. If your coworker cannot be reached, ask someone else in the department for help.

Situation ②

A Mathew Fernsby contacts Bob Peterson on his cellphone to relay Bethany Morton's inquiry. Read the telephone conversation. ◁» 07-4

◎ **Mathew Fernsby** Hello, Bob. This is Mathew Fernsby from the Accounting Department.

◎ **Bob Peterson** Hi, Mathew. How are you doing?

◎ **Mathew Fernsby** I'm great. Thanks. I'm sorry to bother you while you're meeting some clients, but I received a call from the district manager of Universal Fitness.

◎ **Bob Peterson** I see. What was the call about?

◎ **Mathew Fernsby** Well, her name is Bethany Morton. She wants to sell our energy drinks at her clubs.

◎ **Bob Peterson** Oh, that's good news.

◎ **Mathew Fernsby** Yes. She manages twenty clubs. I was planning to deliver the message in person when you're back in the office tomorrow. But I think Universal Fitness could be a big client for us.

◎ **Bob Peterson** No, you were right to contact me. I'll call her right away.

◎ **Mathew Fernsby** Great. Can you take down her number?

◎ **Bob Peterson** Just let me get a pen. Okay, go ahead.

◎ **Mathew Fernsby** It's 905-643-0291.

◎ **Bob Peterson** Got it. Thanks for letting me know.

◎ **Mathew Fernsby** No problem. Have a great day, Bob.

◎ **Bob Peterson** You, too.

Pop-up Questions

1 What is Mr. Peterson currently doing?

2 When was Mr. Fernsby planning to deliver the message?

3 Why does Mr. Fernsby deliver the message today?

4 How will Mr. Peterson contact Ms. Morton?

B **Problem Solving ::** Mathew Fernsby gets a phone call from Bob Peterson, who says the number Mathew gave him is incorrect. Find a partner and choose the roles of Mathew Fernsby and Bob Peterson. Then, role-play to discuss a possible solution. Use the information from Situations 1 and 2 if necessary.

A Let's learn some expressions to use in business.

When greeting someone formally	When greeting someone informally
Hello. How are you doing?	Hey!
Good morning/afternoon.	What's up?
How has everything been with you?	How's it going?
It's nice to see you again.	What's new?
When responding to a greeting	When you need to interrupt someone
I'm great. How about you?	I'm sorry to bother you.
Not bad. Thanks.	I apologize for the interruption.
Not much! You?	Can I bother you for a moment?

B Fill in the blanks with the correct answers from the box. Then, practice the conversation with a partner. ◁ᵸ 07-5

How about you	Not bad. Thanks
How are you doing	I apologize for the interruption

A Hello, Tom. ¹_____?

B I'm great. ²_____?

A ³_____. You're currently out meeting some clients, right?

B That's right. Is there something you need help with?

A Well, ⁴_____, but I just got a call from Carrie Dawson.

B What was the call about?

A She's the manager of Lakeshore Spa. She's interested in selling our products at her spa.

B You were right to contact me. She could be a big client for us.

A I thought so. Can you call her back today?

B Sure. Let me get a pen to write down her number.

Extra Practice

Role-play with your partner. One person delivers a message from a client. The other person agrees to call the client back.

A Hello. How has everything been with you?

B Not bad. Thanks. What's new?

A I'm sorry to bother you, but Linda Zander called to speak to you.

B Thanks for letting me know. I'll call her back today.

Situation ❸

Mathew Fernsby gets an email notifying him of the company's pick for the employee of the month. Read it and see if the results are positive or negative.

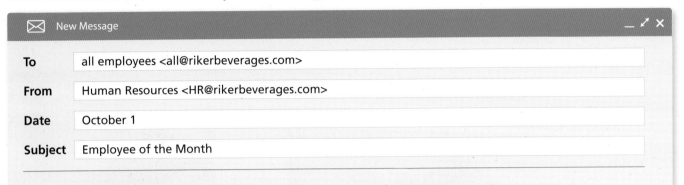

✉ New Message	— ↗ ✕

To	all employees <all@rikerbeverages.com>
From	Human Resources <HR@rikerbeverages.com>
Date	October 1
Subject	Employee of the Month

EMPLOYEE OF THE MONTH

Name: Bob Peterson

Department: Sales

Reason:
I'd like to take this opportunity to recognize Bob Peterson as October's employee of the month. Bob recently closed a deal with Universal Fitness that will allow our company to supply all twenty locations with Riker Beverages products.

Bob also closed a deal with Saint University. Early next year, Riker Beverages will install fifty vending machines on Saint University's downtown campus. Students will be able to purchase our sodas, energy drinks, and new organic juices.

Let's all thank Bob for his hard work and dedication!

Tanya Burnett
Human Resources Manager

Business English Dos and Don'ts

When celebrating the achievements of a colleague, there are some important things to remember. Be formal and specific in announcements. Avoid overly casual phrases.

Dos
- ○ I'd like to take this opportunity to recognize Bob Peterson. (*formal*)
- ○ Sandra Blake was selected as the employee of the month. (*specific*)

Don'ts
- ✗ Bob did an awesome job. (*too casual*)
- ✗ I chose Sandra this time. (*too vague*)

Encourage employees to congratulate one another, but don't be too firm or harsh.

Dos
- ○ Let's all thank Bob for his hard work. (*encouraging*)
- ○ If you see Sandra, congratulate her on a job well done. (*encouraging*)

Don'ts
- ✗ All employees should congratulate Bob by 5:00 P.M. (*too firm*)
- ✗ I expect you to thank Sandra as soon as possible. (*too firm*)

Situation ❶

A Jennifer Davis' coworker, Sandra Burns, is having trouble with some equipment. Read the conversation.

 08-1

J Hey, Sandra. You look frustrated. What's going on?

S I need to copy these contracts, but the copy machine is broken again.

J Oh, really? What's the matter with it now?

S Well, the paper is getting jammed, and the toner smears across the pages. It's such a mess.

J I think I should call the repairman. He's scheduled to come in to install a printer in the lounge. He can probably fix the copy machine then.

S When is he supposed to come?

J Tomorrow at 2:00 P.M.

S Do you think he could come earlier? I really need to copy these contracts.

J I can put in a request. He might have time to stop by this afternoon.

S I hope he can. Otherwise, I'll have to go downtown to the copy store.

J I'll contact him and let you know.

Pop-up Questions

1 Why does Ms. Burns look frustrated?
2 When is the repairman scheduled to come?
3 What does Ms. Burns need to copy?
4 Where might Ms. Burns have to go?

B Take Notes :: Based on the conversation in A, complete the note.

✔ Copy machine is broken (paper is getting ¹ _____ / toner ² _____ across the pages)

✔ Call the repairman (he's scheduled to come ³ _____ at 2:00 P.M.)

✔ Ask if he can come in this ⁴ _____

✔ Let Sandra know if he can fix the copy machine ⁵ _____

Background Knowledge

A Read and learn about how to maintain office equipment.

Office equipment, such as printers, copy machines, and computers, can be expensive to repair. It is even more expensive to replace. It's important to take care of your office's equipment. Doing that will keep it running well for a long time.

Place your equipment in a safe location. Heat and water can damage electronic equipment quickly. Make sure it's not close to heaters or air conditioners. It should be far away from water sources, like sinks and hoses, as well. A cool, dry place is the most suitable.

Clean your equipment regularly. This might include dusting computer parts or removing paper clutter from printers. When you change the toner in your copy machine, some of the toner might spill. Make sure to clean it thoroughly. Additionally, have your equipment serviced regularly. A skilled repairman can make sure it remains in good working order.

Pop-up Questions

1 What can heat and water do to equipment?

2 What should you do if toner spills?

B Listen to the conversation and answer the questions. 08-2

1 **What is wrong with the computer's fans?**

a. They got wet.   b. They are hot.   c. They are dirty.

2 **When is the repairman supposed to update the computers?**

a. today   b. Sunday   c. next week

3 **What might the woman need to do?**

a. retype a report   b. fix a computer   c. delay a deadline

Vocabulary

A Look at the pictures and learn some office equipment.

B Match each office equipment with the problem that can occur.

1 tablet •   • a. cartridge or toner issue

2 laminating machine •   • b. pop-ups appearing

3 shredder •   • c. dull blades

4 printer •   • d. melted pages

5 currency-counting machine •   • e. incorrect amount of money

C Complete the sentences with the words in the box.

copy machine	paper shredder	tablet	heater	air conditioner

1 It's really hot in here. Do you mind if I turn on the _____ ?

2 I'll put some more toner into the _____ .

3 The _____ is quite old, so it's expensive to heat the building.

4 He used a(n) _____ to show us the sales figures.

5 We need to destroy these documents. Put them through the _____ .

Speak Up

Practice the conversation with your partner by using the information in each note. 🔊 08-3

(Example)

Date: June 4

- Computer is broken (pop-ups keep appearing / the screen is freezing)
- Call the repairman (he's scheduled to come next Tuesday at 3:00 P.M.)
- Ask if he can come in tomorrow
- Let Jenny know if he can fix the computer tomorrow

(Note 1)

Date: October 13

- Air conditioner is broken (it's making a loud noise / the air is hot)
- Call the repairman (he's scheduled to come next Friday at 5:00 P.M.)
- Ask if he can come in today
- Let Sam know if he can fix the air conditioner today

(Note 2)

Date: January 5

- Heater is broken (it won't turn on / the office is freezing)
- Call the repairman (he's scheduled to come on Saturday afternoon)
- Ask if he can come in this afternoon
- Let Beth know if he can fix the heater this afternoon

(Note 3)

Date: August 2

- Telephones are broken (we can't make outgoing calls / there's no dial tone)
- Call the repairman (he's scheduled to come this Friday at 10:00 A.M.)
- Ask if he can come in today
- Let Lisa know if he can fix the telephones today

A Hey, Jenny. What's the matter?

B The computer is broken again.

A What's wrong this time?

B Pop-ups keep appearing, and the screen is freezing.

A Oh, I see. The repairman isn't scheduled to come in until next Tuesday at 3:00 P.M.

B Can you call and ask if he can come tomorrow?

A Sure. He might have an opening in his schedule.

B I hope so. I'm not sure I can wait until next week.

A Right. I'll let you know what he says.

B Okay. Thank you!

> **! Tips for Success**
>
> When your coworker is having trouble with some equipment, offer assistance. Offer to call a repairman.

A Let's learn about the passive voice.

Positive / Negative	Interrogative
Use **subject + be verb + (not) past participle** to emphasize the person or object that experiences an action.	Use **be verb + subject + past participle** to ask a question about the person or object that experiences an action.
The computer **is broken**. The contracts **were not sent** last week. The book **was written** by Dr. Henry Fleming.	**Was** this office **built** in 2002? **Were** the computers **updated** over the weekend? **Was** Mr. Black **asked** to sign the contract?

B Complete the following sentences by using the passive forms of the verbs in the parentheses.

1 Currently, the air conditioner _____. (*break*)

2 I think the boxes _____ to him last week. (*deliver*)

3 _____ these products _____ in India? (*make*)

4 The document _____ properly, so I can't open it. (*not + save*)

5 _____ the breakroom _____ yesterday? (*clean*)

6 The menu _____ by the restaurant's head chef yesterday. (*approve*)

7 I haven't hired anyone. _____ Ms. Kelly still _____? (*interest*)

8 The company website _____ last Friday. (*not + fix*)

📶 Know-how *at* Work   How to Put in a Request for Repairs

Servicing equipment is the best way to ensure it stays in working order. However, some repairs are inevitable. There are a few things to remember when putting in a request for repairs.

1 Make a detailed list of all the problems you are experiencing with the equipment. Ask your coworkers to explain the problems they had. This will help the repairman assess the whole machine.

2 If your office uses repair request forms, fill one out detailing the problem. Submit your repair request to your manager for approval.

3 Call the repairman and arrange a time for him to visit your office. Let him know if the repairs are urgent. However, be prepared to wait if he has a busy schedule.

4 When the repairman arrives, explain the problem. Speak to your manager if the repairman suggests replacing a part or purchasing a new machine.

Situation ②

A Jennifer Davis exchanges voicemail messages with the repairman about her office's copy machine. Read the voicemail messages. 🔊 08-4

You have one new message, sent at 10:03 A.M. on August 10.

This is Jennifer Davis calling from the Grove Employment Agency. I know you're planning to visit our office tomorrow at 2:00 P.M., but we're having a lot of trouble with our copy machine. By any chance, do you have time to stop by today to fix it?

It's short notice, so I understand if you can't fit it into your schedule. Tomorrow is fine, too. Please call me back and let me know. My number is 556-743-2231. Thanks, and have a nice day.

You have one new message, sent at 11:22 A.M. on August 10.

Hello, Ms. Davis. This is Timothy Lindon from Ace Tech. I got your message about the copy machine. You're in luck since I just had a cancelation. I will head to your office to install the printer today at 4:00 P.M. While I'm there, I'll have a look at the copy machine as well.

If I remember correctly, your copy machine is a Linear 2000. That's quite an old model. Have you considered getting a new one? My company provides copy machine rentals at affordable prices.

Anyway, see you later today.

Pop-up Questions

1 Where does Ms. Davis work?

2 What does Ms. Davis ask Mr. Lindon to do?

3 When will Mr. Lindon visit Ms. Davis' office?

4 What does Mr. Lindon say about the copy machine?

B **Problem Solving ::** Jennifer Davis decides the copy machine is too old and should be replaced. Find a partner and choose the roles of Jennifer Davis and her manager. Then, role-play to discuss a possible solution. Use the information from the voicemail messages in A if necessary.

 **Useful Expressions**

A **Let's learn some expressions to use in business.**

When asking about the possibility of an action	When confirming or denying possibility
By any chance, do you have time to stop by?	You're in luck since I just had a cancelation.
I don't suppose you could fix it today.	I suppose I could stop by this afternoon.
I wonder if you could install a new printer.	I'm sorry. I can't make time today.
Perhaps you could send the file to her.	Sorry, but my schedule is full tomorrow.
When relaying details you're uncertain about	**When confirming or denying details**
If I remember correctly, it's a Linear 2000.	Yes, that's correct.
If my memory serves me right, the client is based in Chicago.	No, I don't think that's true.
If I'm not mistaken, she was promoted last year.	I'm not sure. I will have to check.

B **Fill in the blanks with the correct answers from the box. Then, practice the conversation with a partner.** 🔊 08-5

Yes, that's correct	Sorry, but my schedule is full today
If my memory serves me right	I don't suppose you could fix it today

A Hello. This is Sue calling from Wild Graphic Designs.

B Hi, Sue. What can I do for you?

A The air conditioner is broken again. [1] _____ .

B [2] _____ . I could stop by tomorrow at 2:00 P.M.

A That would be great. Thank you.

B [3] _____ , your air conditioner is a Swift 8000.

A [4] _____ .

B I see. That's a pretty old model. Have you considered replacing it?

A Hmm, I would have to ask my manager about that.

B It might be cheaper than repairing it so often.

Extra Practice

Role-play with your partner. One person mentions some equipment is broken. The repairman agrees to stop by to repair it.

A The heater is broken again. By any chance, can you stop by to fix it today?

B You're in luck since I just had a cancelation.

A Great! What time will you come?

B I'll head to your office at 3:00 P.M.

Situation 3

Jennifer Davis gets an email from the repairman with a scanned receipt attached. Read it and see if the results are positive or negative.

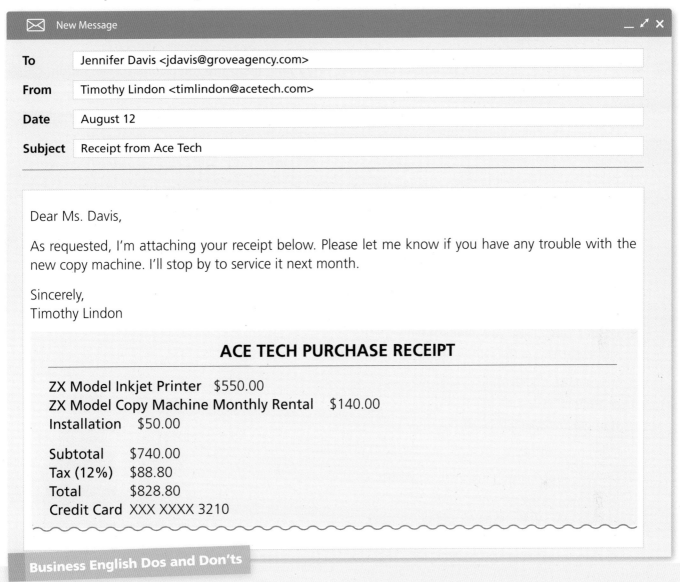

New Message	

To   Jennifer Davis <jdavis@groveagency.com>

From   Timothy Lindon <timlindon@acetech.com>

Date   August 12

Subject   Receipt from Ace Tech

Dear Ms. Davis,

As requested, I'm attaching your receipt below. Please let me know if you have any trouble with the new copy machine. I'll stop by to service it next month.

Sincerely,
Timothy Lindon

ACE TECH PURCHASE RECEIPT

ZX Model Inkjet Printer $550.00
ZX Model Copy Machine Monthly Rental $140.00
Installation $50.00

Subtotal $740.00
Tax (12%) $88.80
Total $828.80
Credit Card   XXX XXXX 3210

Business English Dos and Don'ts

When you need something repaired, there are some important things to remember. Be flexible. Suggest multiple times instead of demanding the work be done today.

Dos	Don'ts
○ Monday or Tuesday would work for us. (*flexible*) ○ Tomorrow will be fine, too. (*flexible*)	✕ You have to come in today. (*demanding*) ✕ I need it repaired immediately. (*demanding*)

Be considerate of a worker's time. Use reassuring phrases rather than selfish statements.

Dos	Don'ts
○ It's short notice, so I understand if you can't. (*considerate*) ○ I know you have a very busy schedule. (*considerate*)	✕ This is such an inconvenience. (*selfish*) ✕ I won't be able to get anything done now. (*selfish*)

Situation 1

A Daniel Yang gets a call from a potential customer, Priya Jain. Read the telephone conversation. 🔊 09-1

> 🎧 **Daniel Yang** Hello. You've reached Little Bear Publishing. This is Daniel Yang speaking. How can I help you?
>
> 🎧 **Priya Jain** Hello. I recently opened my own tutoring business, and I'm interested in purchasing books for my students.
>
> 🎧 **Daniel Yang** Okay. What subjects will you be teaching?
>
> 🎧 **Priya Jain** Math and geography mostly.
>
> 🎧 **Daniel Yang** I see. Are your students all the same age, or are they different ages?
>
> 🎧 **Priya Jain** Well, they're mostly high schoolers. However, I've had some special requests to open classes to sixth graders as well.
>
> 🎧 **Daniel Yang** Okay. I think you might be interested in our *Learning Scape* series. It covers two subjects, math and geography, and targets high school students. There are five levels in each subject.
>
> 🎧 **Priya Jain** That sounds great. Do you have any books for younger students?
>
> 🎧 **Daniel Yang** The *Learning Scape Beginner* series is appropriate for sixth graders. There are three levels per subject.
>
> 🎧 **Priya Jain** All right. Can you send me a sample of each book? That way, I can choose the right levels.
>
> 🎧 **Daniel Yang** Sure. Let me know your address, and I'll ship them to you today.

Read more

Pop-up Questions

1 What type of business did Ms. Jain recently open?
2 What subjects does Ms. Jain teach?
3 What series does Mr. Yang recommend for high schoolers?
4 What does Ms. Jain ask Mr. Yang to send?

B Take Notes :: Based on the telephone conversation in A, complete the invoice.

	Description	Quantity	Unit Price	Total
1	Learning Scape Bundle (Level 1 to [1] _____ – Math and [2] _____)	1	$111.00	$111.00
2	Learning Scape [3] _____ Bundle (Level 1 to [4] _____ – same as above)	1	$77.98	$77.98
Samples Requested By: [5] _____				Total: $188.98

Background Knowledge

Ⓐ Read and learn about how to send a sample.

Samples help businesses choose which products to sell. As a seller, you can send samples to a buyer. The buyer checks the quality and the price of each sample. If both are satisfactory, he or she will place an order. These items are then sold to customers.

Before sending samples, remember to mark the products. You might need to tear or cut clothing samples. You should stamp shoes and books with ink. These markings ensure that the samples are not sold to customers. Send the samples along with an invoice.

A good invoice lists all of the items and their prices. It has item descriptions as well as tax information. Even though samples are free, you should still send an invoice. This is especially true for samples that travel overseas. Otherwise, customs may not allow the samples into the country.

Pop-up Questions

1 What do samples help businesses do?

2 What must sellers do before sending samples?

Ⓑ Listen to the voicemail and answer the questions. 🔊 09-2

1 **Who recently opened a clothing shop?**

   a. Joshua   b. William   c. Jane

2 **What does William want to send?**

   a. new accessories   b. some fall clothing   c. furniture

3 **What does William NOT remind Joshua to do?**

   a. ship a product   b. mark some samples   c. include an invoice

Vocabulary

A Look at the invoice and fill in the blanks with the correct words from the box.

| zip code | description | logo | unit price | total | quantity | client address |

INVOICE

1 _____

San's Flooring
32 Crescent Lane
Auckland, NZ, 0602   2 _____
520-444-0607
orders@sansflooring.com

Ship To:
Baker Design
5 Shell Drive, 13th Floor   3 _____
Auckland, NZ, 0603

4	5	6	7
Marble Tile (gray)	1	$11.99	$11.99
Granite Tile (beige)	1	$12.99	$12.99
Ceramic Tile (white)	1	$9.99	$9.99
			$34.97

B Complete the sentences with the words in the box.

| unit price | total | client address | invoice | description |

1 He placed a(n) _____ in the box with the sample.

2 The _____ for each chair is $59.99.

3 Your order _____ comes to $309.59 with tax.

4 Please paste the _____ on the top of the box.

5 Can you add the colors to each _____ on the invoice?

Speak Up

Practice the conversation with your partner by using the information on each invoice. 🔊 09-3

Example

	Description	Quantity	Unit Price	Total
1	Bedsheets Single Size (ice blue)	1	$49.99	$49.99
2	Bedsheets Single Size (forest green)	1	$45.99	$45.99
3	Bedsheets Single Size (ivory)	1	$48.99	$48.99
	Samples Requested By: Candice Lay of Bed Bath and Wonder			**$144.97**

A Hello. This is Candice Lay from Bed Bath and Wonder.

B Hi, Ms. Lay. What can I do for you?

A I'm interested in selling some of your products at my store.

B That's great to hear. Which products are you interested in?

A I'm mostly looking for bedsheets.

B I could send you some samples if you like.

A Sure. That would help a lot.

B Okay. I'll send you some of our bestsellers.

A Great. How much will that cost?

B Well, the bedsheets I'm sending are normally under 50 dollars each. However, the samples are free.

! Tips for Success

When a potential customer does not know which products to order, offer to send samples of products he or she may like.

Invoice 1

	Description	Quantity	Unit Price	Total
1	Women's Ankle Boots (beige)	1	$89.99	$89.99
2	Men's Hiking Boots (black)	1	$87.99	$87.99
3	Boy's Winter Boots (navy)	1	$64.99	$64.99
	Samples Requested By: Tom Wang of Tom's Shoes			**$242.97**

Invoice 2

	Description	Quantity	Unit Price	Total
1	Modern Bar Stool (black)	1	$139.99	$139.99
2	Padded Rocking Chair (gray)	1	$149.99	$149.99
3	Reclining Desk Chair (blue)	1	$122.99	$122.99
	Samples Requested By: Jason Wexler of the Stetson Furniture Company			**$412.97**

 **GRAMMAR**

A Let's learn about wh-questions.

what	asking for information	**What** is your favorite food?
when	asking for a time	**When** is the conference?
where	asking for a place	**Where** can he get a parking pass?
who	asking about a person or people	**Who** sent the packages last week?
whose	asking about ownership	**Whose** office are we meeting in?
which	asking about a choice	**Which** brand do you want to order?
why	asking for a reason	**Why** was the client upset?
how	asking about quality or method	**How** did he fix the printer?

B Complete the following sentences by using the correct wh-question word.

1 A .... spoke to Mr. Bradley on the phone?
  B Jenny spoke to him.

2 A .... will he take his vacation?
  B Maybe this month or next month.

3 A .... did we have the product launch party?
  B I think it was at a hotel.

4 A .... computer is that?
  B That's Mr. West's computer.

5 A .... one do you like, the red or blue one?
  B I like the blue one.

6 A .... is her phone number?
  B It's 555-3423.

7 A .... will you get to the exhibition?
  B I'll probably take a taxi there.

8 A .... did he cancel the meeting?
  B He's sick, so he stayed home.

Know-how at Work   **How to Ensure an Order is Correct**

Making sure customers get the products they ordered on time is important for your business. Mistakes can lead to angry customers. You might lose their business. There are a few ways to make sure orders are correct.

1 If you're taking an order by phone or email, record the item numbers and the quantities. Double-check that all the information is correct.

2 Before you ship the order, prepare a detailed invoice. Make sure the invoice matches your order records. If some items are missing, revise your invoice.

3 Make sure the items match the invoice exactly. Compare product numbers, descriptions, and quantities. Remove any items the customer did not order. Add items that are missing to the box.

4 Once you've checked the order, seal the box with the invoice inside. This will prevent the order from being tampered with.

Situation ②

A Daniel Yang gets an email from Priya Jain in response to the samples he sent. Read the email.

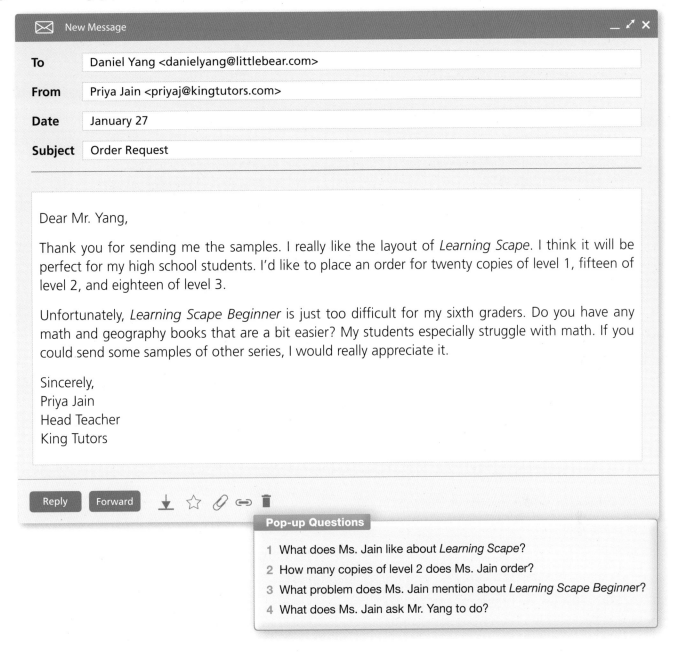

✉ New Message

To	Daniel Yang <danielyang@littlebear.com>
From	Priya Jain <priyaj@kingtutors.com>
Date	January 27
Subject	Order Request

Dear Mr. Yang,

Thank you for sending me the samples. I really like the layout of *Learning Scape*. I think it will be perfect for my high school students. I'd like to place an order for twenty copies of level 1, fifteen of level 2, and eighteen of level 3.

Unfortunately, *Learning Scape Beginner* is just too difficult for my sixth graders. Do you have any math and geography books that are a bit easier? My students especially struggle with math. If you could send some samples of other series, I would really appreciate it.

Sincerely,
Priya Jain
Head Teacher
King Tutors

Reply   Forward   ↓ ☆ 🔗 ⊝ 🗑

Pop-up Questions

1 What does Ms. Jain like about *Learning Scape*?

2 How many copies of level 2 does Ms. Jain order?

3 What problem does Ms. Jain mention about *Learning Scape Beginner*?

4 What does Ms. Jain ask Mr. Yang to do?

B **Problem Solving ::** Daniel Yang must call Priya Jain to let her know that the level-3 books are currently out of stock. Find a partner and choose the roles of Daniel Yang and Priya Jain. Then, role-play to discuss a possible solution. Use the information from the email in A if necessary.

 **Useful Expressions**

A Let's learn some expressions to use in business.

When emphasizing an opinion or decision	When you understand or find out something
My students especially struggle with math.	I see.
I really like the layout of *Learning Scape*.	All right.
He completely ruined our presentation.	Got it.
We certainly cannot change the location.	Understood.
When answering the phone	**When asking a customer to wait on the phone**
You've reached Little Bear Publishing.	Hold for a moment, please.
Thank you for calling Roth Accounting.	Can I put you on hold for a minute?
This is Daniel Yang speaking.	Just a moment. I'll transfer you.

B Fill in the blanks with the correct answers from the box. Then, practice the conversation with a partner. ◀)) 09-4

understood	can I put you on hold for a minute
you've reached Curtains Unlimited	my customers especially love pastel colors

A Hello. ¹ _____.

B Hi. I'm interested in selling your curtains at my store.

A Certainly. ² _____?

B Sure. No problem.

A Sorry about that. You mentioned you're interested in curtains.

B Yes, I own a home furnishing store.

A Is there anything specific you're looking for?

B Well, ³ _____.

A ⁴ _____. We have a new line of pastels and florals.

B That sounds perfect. Can you send me some samples?

A Sure. Just let me know your store's address.

Extra Practice

Role-play with your partner. One person inquires about selling some products. The other person suggests a new line of products.

A Hello. You've reached Boots Are Us. How can I help you?

B Hi. I'm interested in selling your boots at my store.

A All right. We have a new line of winter boots.

B Great. Can you send me some samples?

Situation ③

Daniel Yang sees a review of his company written by Priya Jain. Read it and see if the results are positive or negative.

Little Bear Publishing – Reviews

Priya Jain
★★★★★ *2 weeks ago*
Great Service, Excellent Products

My experience with Little Bear Publishing has been excellent thus far. Recently, I opened my own tutoring company. Little Bear Publishing sent me numerous samples and helped me choose the right books for my students.

Daniel Yang was especially courteous and helpful. When the books I needed were out of stock, Mr. Yang went out of his way to suggest similar products. He even offered a discount on my order to apologize for the trouble. Thanks to him, my tutoring business is running smoothly. I highly recommend Little Bear Publishing to educators.

Business English Dos and Don'ts

When you are reviewing a product, service, or business positively, there are a few things to remember. Give clear reasons why you are recommending the item or the business.

Dos
- ○ Little Bear Publishing helped me choose the right books. (*reason*)
- ○ Daniel Yang was especially courteous and helpful. (*reason*)

Don'ts
- ✕ Little Bear Publishing is great. (*too vague*)
- ✕ Daniel Yang does a lot. (*too vague*)

Repeat your recommendation generally at the end of your review. Try not to add new details.

Dos
- ○ I highly recommend Little Bear Publishing. (*recommendation*)
- ○ I recommend this service to educators. (*recommendation*)

Don'ts
- ✕ I was glad to get my samples on time. (*detail*)
- ✕ I think chapter 1 is very interesting. (*detail*)

Situation ❶

A Kit Patterson gets an email from his boss inviting him to a conference. Read the email and the forwarded invitation.

New Message	— ↗ ✕

To	Kit Patterson <kpatterson@pierceenterprises.com>
From	Jack Morales <jackmorales@pierceenterprises.com>
Date	May 12
Subject	[FWD] International Business Conference

Hi, Kit,

I won't be able to attend the Los Angeles International Business Conference this year. I'd like you and Janet Hunter to fly there instead and meet with potential clients. I'm forwarding you the information now. You need to book flights and hotel rooms and also rent a car in advance.

Jack Morales
Senior Manager

--------------------Forwarded message------------------------

To: Jack Morales <jackmorales@pierceenterprises.com>
From: Dorothy Brown <dbrown@internationalbusinessconference.com>
Date: May 11
Subject: International Business Conference

Dear Mr. Morales,

I'm pleased to invite you to the annual Los Angeles International Business Conference. The conference will be held at the West Exhibition Center in Los Angeles from July 10 to 13.

To confirm your attendance, please register at www.internationalbusinessconference.com. Make sure to add your name, address, email, and phone number. Please also indicate the number of attendees.

We look forward to seeing you this year!

Best Regards,
Dorothy Brown

REPLY **FORWARD**

Pop-up Questions

1 What was Mr. Morales invited to?

2 Who will go in Mr. Morales' place?

3 What city is the conference in?

4 How can guests confirm their attendance?

B **Take Notes ::** Based on the email in A, complete the memo.

> Event: international business conference / to meet with ¹ _____
>
> Date: ² _____
>
> Location: ³ _____
>
> Attendees : Kit Patterson and ⁴ _____
>
> To Do:
> - Register at www.internationalbusinessconference.com
> - Book ⁵ _____
> - Rent a car in advance

Background Knowledge

A **Read and learn about how to plan a business trip.**

Business trips can help companies gain new clients or finalize business deals. Planning ahead will make the trip less stressful. Start by booking your flight in advance. Try not to book a late flight. If it gets delayed, you might have to wait until the next day to travel.

You can book a hotel ahead of time, too. Choose a hotel that isn't too far from the places you will visit. Take note of the check-in and checkout times. You can also rent a car in advance. This is a good idea if you are familiar with the area.

Make sure to pack everything you will need for your trip. Bring your ID, passport, business cards, laptop computer, and any company documents you'll need. Pack business clothing as well as casual clothes for sightseeing. But don't bring too much, or you'll have to check your luggage. Checked luggage might get lost.

Pop-up Questions

1 What might happen if you book a late flight?

2 What might get lost during a flight?

B **Listen to the conversation and answer the questions.** 🔊 10-1

1 **Who received the invitation first?**

a. Molly   b. Frederick   c. Janice

2 **Where will the event take place?**

a. at the Grand Valley Resort   b. at the Holiday Hotel   c. at London Center

3 **What does Molly say the Holiday Hotel has?**

a. a friendly staff   b. great reviews   c. excellent food

Vocabulary

Ⓐ Look at the pictures and learn some words related to business trips.

Items

business card | passport | boarding pass | charger | luggage

Activities

book a flight/hotel room | attend a meeting | rent a car | get a receipt

Ⓑ Complete the sentences with the words in the box.

rent a car	luggage	attend a meeting	charger
business card	book a hotel room	get a receipt	boarding pass

1 He will fly to Germany. He will _____ with the customer.

2 She gave me her _____. Her name and phone number are on it.

3 Don't bring too much _____. The airline might lose it.

4 Let's _____. It's cheaper than taking taxis.

5 Pay for the client's dinner. _____ from the restaurant.

6 Your phone battery might die. Bring a _____.

7 You should _____. Choose one close to the airport.

8 The passenger showed his _____. Then, he boarded the plane.

82

Speak Up

Practice the conversation with your partner by using the information in each memo. 🔊 10-2

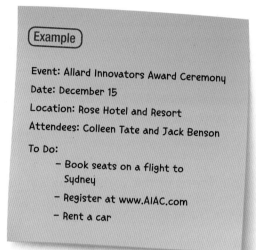

Example

Event: Allard Innovators Award Ceremony

Date: December 15

Location: Rose Hotel and Resort

Attendees: Colleen Tate and Jack Benson

To Do:
- Book seats on a flight to Sydney
- Register at www.AIAC.com
- Rent a car

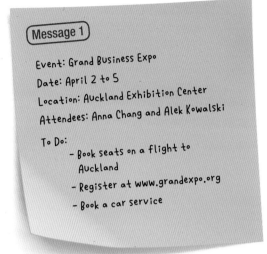

Message 1

Event: Grand Business Expo

Date: April 2 to 5

Location: Auckland Exhibition Center

Attendees: Anna Chang and Alek Kowalski

To Do:
- Book seats on a flight to Auckland
- Register at www.grandexpo.org
- Book a car service

Message 2

Event: West Technology Tradeshow

Date: June 25 to 26

Location: Prince Convention Center

Attendees: Dylan Marlow and Tanya Sim

To Do:
- Book seats on a flight to Ottawa
- Register at www.westontradeshow.com
- Rent a car

Message 3

Event: Sanderson Company Product Launch

Date: May 26

Location: Sanderson Company Headquarters

Attendees: Elly Tanaka and Karl Schmidt

To Do:
- Book seats on a flight to Beijing
- Register at www.sandersonlaunch.org
- Book a limo service

A Hi, Colleen. I just got an email from Mr. Lewis.

B Hey, Jack. What did he say?

A He got invited to the Allard Innovators Award Ceremony.

B Wow. That's exciting.

A Yeah, he'd like us to go with him.

B Okay, sure. When is it?

A It's December 15 at the Rose Hotel and Resort.

B That's in Sydney, right? We'll have to book seats on a flight there.

A Yes. We should also rent a car.

B Of course. I'll look into it right away.

! Tips for Success

Sometimes you must travel on business with your coworkers. Offer to help book seats on flights or hotel rooms and to arrange transportation.

 **GRAMMAR**

A Let's learn about participle adjectives.

Present	Past
Use **verb + -ing** as an adjective to describe people or things that cause emotions.	Use **verb + -ed** as an adjective to describe emotions that people feel.
Patricia's presentation was **exciting**.	I am **excited** about her ideas.
The news was so **shocking**.	Mr. Hunt was **shocked** by the news.
His complaints are **surprising**.	We are **surprised** by his complaints.

B Complete the following sentences by using the participle forms of the verbs in the parentheses.

1 We were _____ when we heard about the hurricane. (*shock*)

2 The manager is not _____ about this year's budget. (*worry*)

3 They said the company dinner was _____. (*bore*)

4 Organizing a big company event is _____. (*challenge*)

5 Last year's sales figures were very _____. (*disappoint*)

6 Sally's hard work and great attitude are _____. (*inspire*)

7 Jane and Marcus were _____ after they got fired. (*depress*)

8 Mr. Addison was not _____ by our presentation. (*impress*)

📶 Know-how *at* Work   How to Reschedule a Business Trip

Unexpected changes to your business trip can be frustrating. The date of an event might change, or a client might request a change in a schedule. As a result, there may be a few things you must reschedule.

1 If you plan to fly, call the airline first. Ask about booking a different flight. However, you might have to pay a fee to change your reservation.

2 Next, call the hotel. Ask about changing your reservation. If there aren't any rooms available, call other hotels. Book a room elsewhere and cancel your original reservation.

3 If you made restaurant reservations, you might have to change them as well. Ask your clients about the best time to meet. Call the restaurants to reschedule.

4 Inform your manager and coworkers of your new departure and return dates. That way, your department can prepare for your absence.

Situation ②

A **Kit Patterson gets an email from Dorothy Brown explaining a change of plans. Read the email.**

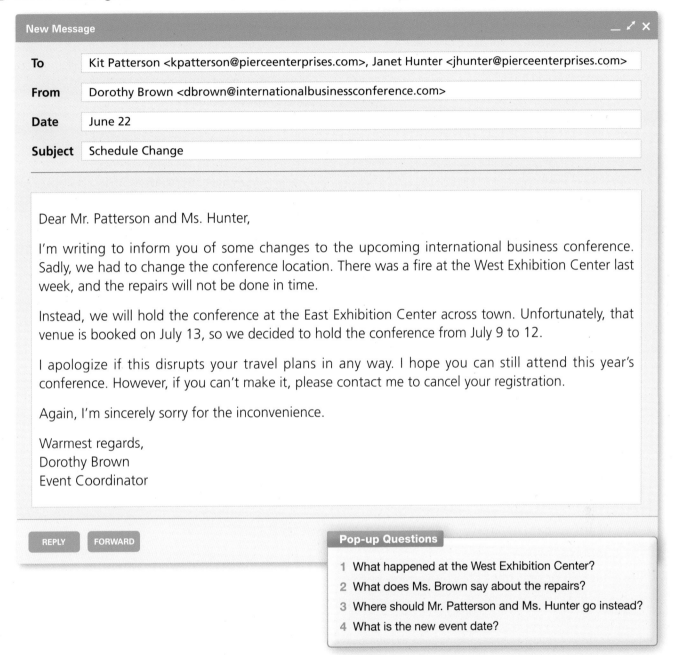

New Message — ↗ ✕

To	Kit Patterson <kpatterson@pierceenterprises.com>, Janet Hunter <jhunter@pierceenterprises.com>
From	Dorothy Brown <dbrown@internationalbusinessconference.com>
Date	June 22
Subject	Schedule Change

Dear Mr. Patterson and Ms. Hunter,

I'm writing to inform you of some changes to the upcoming international business conference. Sadly, we had to change the conference location. There was a fire at the West Exhibition Center last week, and the repairs will not be done in time.

Instead, we will hold the conference at the East Exhibition Center across town. Unfortunately, that venue is booked on July 13, so we decided to hold the conference from July 9 to 12.

I apologize if this disrupts your travel plans in any way. I hope you can still attend this year's conference. However, if you can't make it, please contact me to cancel your registration.

Again, I'm sincerely sorry for the inconvenience.

Warmest regards,
Dorothy Brown
Event Coordinator

REPLY   FORWARD

Pop-up Questions

1 What happened at the West Exhibition Center?
2 What does Ms. Brown say about the repairs?
3 Where should Mr. Patterson and Ms. Hunter go instead?
4 What is the new event date?

B **Problem Solving :: Kit Patterson must call the airline to reschedule his flight. Find a partner and choose the roles of Kit Patterson and the airline employee. Then, role-play to discuss a possible solution. Use the information from the email in A if necessary.**

 **Useful Expressions**

A **Let's learn some expressions to use in business.**

When informing someone of a change of plans	When expressing regret about a change of plans
I'm writing to inform you of some changes. I'm calling to let you know about a change of plans. I'm contacting you because your meeting was canceled. My manager asked me to call you about a cancelation.	Sadly, we had to change the location. Unfortunately, that venue is booked. Regrettably, the reservation can't be changed. Regretfully, we can't reschedule the conference.
When encouraging someone to attend an event	When apologizing for a serious disruption
I hope you can still attend this year's conference. We hope you can reschedule your flight. We'd really like it if you could still join us.	I apologize if this disrupts your travel plans. I'm sincerely sorry for the inconvenience. We feel awful about this situation.

B **Fill in the blanks with the correct answers from the box. Then, practice the conversation with a partner.** ◀)) 10-3

Sadly, we had to change the date I hope you can still attend	I'm sincerely sorry for the inconvenience I'm calling to let you know about some changes

A Hello. This is Sylvia Major calling.

B Hi, Ms. Major. How can I help you?

A ¹ _____ to the Leaders of Tomorrow Expo.

B I see. What sort of changes?

A ² _____. The venue needs some unexpected repairs.

B That's too bad. What's the new date?

A It's November 14. ³ _____.

B I'm not sure if I can reschedule my flight, but I will try.

A I understand. ⁴ _____.

B That's all right. Thanks for letting me know.

A Of course. Contact me if you have any questions or concerns.

Extra Practice

Role-play with your partner. One person mentions a change of plans to an event. The other person promises to try to attend the event.

A I'm contacting you because the event was postponed.

B That's too bad. What's the new date?

A It's July 3. I hope you can still attend.

B I'm not sure if I can reschedule my trip, but I will try.

Situation ③

Kit Patterson gets a call from Carole Fritz in the Accounting Department in response to the expense report he submitted. Read it and see if the results are positive or negative. 🔊 10-4

Carole Fritz Hi, Kit. This is Carole from Accounting. How was your business trip?

Kit Patterson Well, rescheduling everything was tough, but the conference was fantastic. I really enjoyed it.

Carole Fritz That's great to hear. So I got your trip expense report yesterday.

Kit Patterson Right. Is there anything else I need to submit?

Carole Fritz I have receipts for your flights, hotel, rental car, and meals. However, I don't see any receipts for gas.

Kit Patterson Yes. I misplaced the gas receipts.

Carole Fritz Oh, you lost them? As you know, it's company policy to submit all receipts. Otherwise, the expenses won't be reimbursed.

Kit Patterson That's disappointing to hear.

Carole Fritz Yes. I'm sorry to have to tell you this, but the rules are clear. Unfortunately, we can't bend them this time.

Kit Patterson I understand. I'll be more careful in the future.

Carole Fritz The rest of your report looks good. I will add the amount to your next paycheck.

Kit Patterson Thanks, Carole. Have a nice day.

Business English Dos and Don'ts

When you deliver bad news to a coworker or customer, there are some important things to remember. Use an apologetic tone as well as apologetic phrases. Try not to be too harsh.

Dos
- ○ I'm sorry to have to tell you this. (*apologetic*)
- ○ Unfortunately, we can't bend the rules this time. (*apologetic*)

Don'ts
- ✕ It's your job to know the rules. (*harsh*)
- ✕ Don't expect any special treatment. (*harsh*)

Explain the bad news clearly. Don't be vague about rules or obligations.

Dos
- ○ It's company policy to submit all receipts. (*clear*)
- ○ The application deadline has already passed. (*clear*)

Don'ts
- ✕ You violated a policy. (*not specific*)
- ✕ You didn't apply properly. (*not specific*)

Situation ❶

Ⓐ **Mitch Vance gets a message in the company group chat informing him of an upcoming event. Read the instant message chain.**

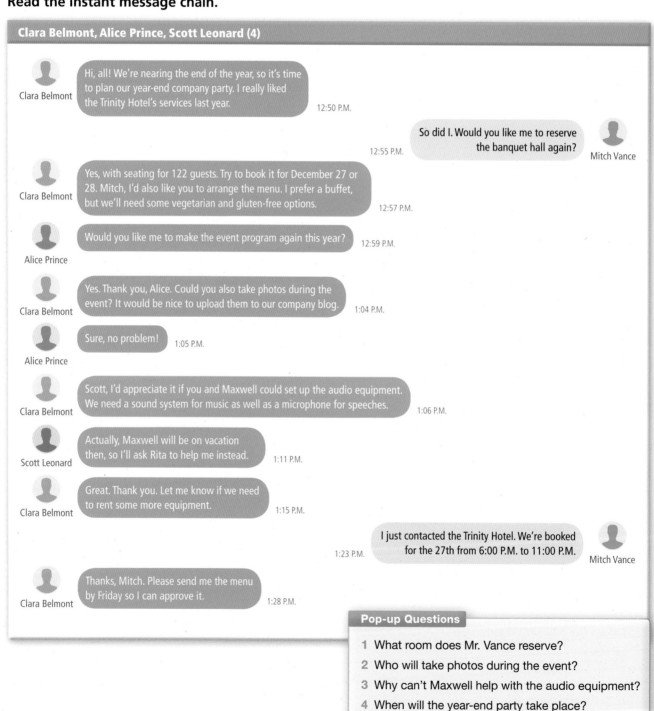

Clara Belmont, Alice Prince, Scott Leonard (4)

Clara Belmont: Hi, all! We're nearing the end of the year, so it's time to plan our year-end company party. I really liked the Trinity Hotel's services last year. — 12:50 P.M.

Mitch Vance: So did I. Would you like me to reserve the banquet hall again? — 12:55 P.M.

Clara Belmont: Yes, with seating for 122 guests. Try to book it for December 27 or 28. Mitch, I'd also like you to arrange the menu. I prefer a buffet, but we'll need some vegetarian and gluten-free options. — 12:57 P.M.

Alice Prince: Would you like me to make the event program again this year? — 12:59 P.M.

Clara Belmont: Yes. Thank you, Alice. Could you also take photos during the event? It would be nice to upload them to our company blog. — 1:04 P.M.

Alice Prince: Sure, no problem! — 1:05 P.M.

Clara Belmont: Scott, I'd appreciate it if you and Maxwell could set up the audio equipment. We need a sound system for music as well as a microphone for speeches. — 1:06 P.M.

Scott Leonard: Actually, Maxwell will be on vacation then, so I'll ask Rita to help me instead. — 1:11 P.M.

Clara Belmont: Great. Thank you. Let me know if we need to rent some more equipment. — 1:15 P.M.

Mitch Vance: I just contacted the Trinity Hotel. We're booked for the 27th from 6:00 P.M. to 11:00 P.M. — 1:23 P.M.

Clara Belmont: Thanks, Mitch. Please send me the menu by Friday so I can approve it. — 1:28 P.M.

Pop-up Questions

1 What room does Mr. Vance reserve?

2 Who will take photos during the event?

3 Why can't Maxwell help with the audio equipment?

4 When will the year-end party take place?

Ⓑ **Take Notes :: Based on the instant message chain in A, complete the memo.**

Event – ¹ _____ Company Party

Date/Time: ² _____

Location: Trinity Hotel – Banquet Hall

Number of Guests: ³ _____

To Do:

- Mitch – Arrange the menu (buffet with ⁴ _____ options)
- Alice – Make the ⁵ _____ / take photos
- Scott and Rita – ⁶ _____

Background Knowledge

Ⓐ **Read and learn about how to plan a work party.**

Most companies have a few events per year. These include holiday parties, product launches, and fundraisers. Events help employees celebrate successes. They also help build professional relationships. You might get asked to plan a company event. There are a few things to consider.

First, think about the size of the event. If your event is small, you can hold it at a restaurant. Book a hotel or hall if it's a larger event. Send invitations to everyone in the office. Mention the date, the time, and the dress code. Next, plan a great menu. Buffets are affordable, and they have a variety of foods. Think about dietary restrictions and include dishes for everyone.

Finally, plan the entertainment. Some events include speeches, and others have music. Make sure there is audio equipment at the venue. Hire a photographer or ask an employee to take photos of the event. These photos look great on a company blog.

Pop-up Questions

1 What do events help employees do?

2 What should you mention on an invitation?

Ⓑ **Listen to the voicemail and answer the questions.** 🔊 11-1

1 **Who is retiring from the company?**

a. Christopher Marshall   b. Rochelle Vincente   c. Barbara Fields

2 **What dietary option does Mr. Marshall mention?**

a. vegetarian   b. vegan   c. gluten-free

3 **Where will the event likely be held?**

a. at the office   b. at a hotel   c. at a restaurant

Vocabulary

Ⓐ Look at the pictures and learn some words related to work parties.

Dietary Options

Types of Business Parties

Ⓑ Match each word with the correct definition.

1 year-end party •

2 fundraiser •

3 awards ceremony •

4 retirement party •

5 vegetarian •

6 dairy-free •

7 holiday party •

8 nut-free •

• a. a party that celebrates an employee's career

• b. an event at which awards are given

• c. food that does not contain milk, cheese, etc.

• d. food that does not contain any nuts

• e. an event held at the end of the year

• f. food that does not contain meat

• g. a celebration, such as a Christmas party

• h. an event held to raise money

Speak Up

Practice the conversation with your partner by using the information in each memo. 🔊 11-2

Example

Event: holiday party

Number of Guests: 12

Date: December 22

Time: 7:00 to 11:00 P.M.

Location: Wesley's Grill House

Dietary Options: dairy-free

Special Request: reserve the restaurant's party room

Memo 1

Event: product launch party

Number of Guests: 300

Date: March 24

Time: 9:00 to 11:00 P.M.

Location: the Pearl Hotel banquet hall

Dietary Options: gluten-free

Special Request: hire a photographer for the event

Memo 2

Event: retirement party

Number of Guests: 30

Date: September 12

Time: 6:00 to 9:00 P.M.

Location: the Lakeside Seafood Grill

Dietary Options: vegetarian

Special Request: get a cake from Bella's Bakery

Memo 3

Event: awards ceremony

Number of Guests: 155

Date: November 28

Time: 6:30 to 10:00 P.M.

Location: the Felicity Resort banquet hall

Dietary Options: nut-free

Special Request: set up the audio equipment

A Hey, Sam. It's time to plan our holiday party.

B Oh, right. I really liked Wesley's Grill House last year.

A Me, too. Let's book it for 12 guests.

B Sure. Would December 22 be okay?

A That's perfect. I think from 7:00 to 11:00 P.M. would be good.

B Okay. I'll call to set it up.

A Can you make sure there are dairy-free options, too?

B No problem. Anything else?

A Yes. I think we should reserve the restaurant's party room.

B That's a good idea. I'll take care of it.

> **! Tips for Success**
>
> When planning a company event, consider the dietary needs of those attending. Ask the venue about special meal options.

A **Let's learn about *it* as an impersonal pronoun.**

The Impersonal Pronoun It		
Use **it** as the subject to an impersonal verb.	Use **it** to refer to things and animals that were already mentioned.	Use **it** to begin a sentence when the subject is an infinitive.
It's raining. **It**'s 5:50 P.M. **It**'s Sunday, January 2. **It**'s always cold here.	**It**'s a new training program. **It**'s behind the shopping center. **It**'s an amazing product. **It**'s on the receptionist's desk.	**It**'s time to plan our holiday party. **It**'s easy to apply for the class online. **It**'s dangerous to drive during a storm. **It**'s polite to open the door for clients.

B **Complete the sentences with the words in the box. Change the forms of the verbs to the infinitive.**

walk	get	send	choose	make	ask	interrupt	rent

1 It's important _____ an invoice to the customer.

2 It's good _____ for time off in advance.

3 It's easy _____ a restaurant reservation.

4 It's time _____ the employee of the month.

5 It's expensive _____ an office downtown.

6 It's dangerous _____ alone at night.

7 It's rude _____ the manager when he is speaking.

8 It's wonderful _____ a promotion.

🔊 Know-how *at* Work   **How to Plan a Menu**

Food is an important part of a company event. Some events include a meal while others include only light refreshments. Choosing the right foods can make your event successful.

1 If your event includes a meal, you will need to choose what type of meal to offer. Three-course dinners are great for large galas. Buffets are also a good option. They offer a wide variety of foods.

2 If your event does not include a meal, you still might want to serve some refreshments. Drinks, desserts, and appetizers will keep your guests happy.

3 Think about the ingredients when you choose the foods. Consider the dietary needs of your guests. Some of your guests might be vegetarians. Others might need gluten-free, dairy-free, or nut-free options.

4 You should also serve beverages at your event. Include a self-serve drink station or hire a bartender to serve drinks to your guests.

Situation ②

A **Mitch Vance gets an email confirming his company's reservation. Read the hotel reservation confirmation.**

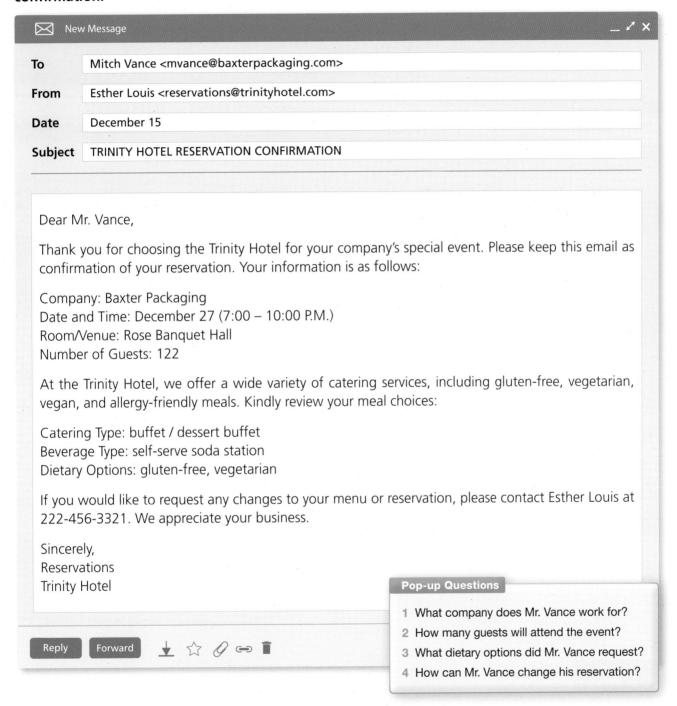

✉ New Message   — ↗ ✕

To	Mitch Vance <mvance@baxterpackaging.com>
From	Esther Louis <reservations@trinityhotel.com>
Date	December 15
Subject	TRINITY HOTEL RESERVATION CONFIRMATION

Dear Mr. Vance,

Thank you for choosing the Trinity Hotel for your company's special event. Please keep this email as confirmation of your reservation. Your information is as follows:

Company: Baxter Packaging
Date and Time: December 27 (7:00 – 10:00 P.M.)
Room/Venue: Rose Banquet Hall
Number of Guests: 122

At the Trinity Hotel, we offer a wide variety of catering services, including gluten-free, vegetarian, vegan, and allergy-friendly meals. Kindly review your meal choices:

Catering Type: buffet / dessert buffet
Beverage Type: self-serve soda station
Dietary Options: gluten-free, vegetarian

If you would like to request any changes to your menu or reservation, please contact Esther Louis at 222-456-3321. We appreciate your business.

Sincerely,
Reservations
Trinity Hotel

Reply   Forward   ↓ ☆ 🖉 🔗 🗑

Pop-up Questions

1 What company does Mr. Vance work for?
2 How many guests will attend the event?
3 What dietary options did Mr. Vance request?
4 How can Mr. Vance change his reservation?

B **Problem Solving ::** The event time noted in the reservation confirmation is incorrect. Mitch Vance must call Esther Louis to change the event time. Find a partner and choose the roles of Mitch Vance and Esther Louis. Then, role-play to discuss a possible solution. Use the information from Situations 1 and 2 if necessary.

 **Useful Expressions**

A **Let's learn some expressions to use in business.**

When giving a customer instructions	When highlighting a service or feature
Please keep this email as confirmation of your reservation.	At the Trinity Hotel, we offer a wide variety of catering services.
If you'd like to make any changes, please contact Helen Mason.	We believe in providing our guests with outstanding service.
Make sure to print your itinerary prior to check-in.	Here at Walter Financial, we handle all your company's finance needs.
Kindly review your meal choices.	

When thanking a customer	When ending a business email or letter
Thank you for choosing the Trinity Hotel.	Sincerely
We appreciate your business.	Regards
Thank you for your continued patronage.	Yours truly

B **Fill in the blanks with the correct answers from the box. Then, practice the conversation with a partner.** 🔊 11-3

please keep it as confirmation	thank you for choosing the Westhill Resort
we offer a wide variety of catering options	if you'd like to make any other changes

A ¹ _____. This is Melissa speaking.

B Hello. My company is having an awards ceremony at your hotel.

A I see. You reserved the banquet hall for the 17th of July?

B That's right. I need to change the number of guests to 200.

A Okay, I'm updating your reservation.

B Thanks. I still need to plan the menu as well.

A At the Westhill Resort, ² _____.

B I think a buffet would be best. We need some vegetarian dishes, too.

A Certainly. I'll email your new reservation. ³ _____.

B Okay. Great.

A ⁴ _____, please contact me.

B Thanks a lot.

Extra Practice

Role-play with your partner. One person asks to change a reservation. The other person agrees to make the change.

A Thank you for choosing the Seashore Restaurant.

B This is Becky Hill. I'd like to change my reservation from 6:00 P.M. to 7:00 P.M.

A Okay. If you'd like to make any other changes, please call me.

B Great. Thanks a lot.

Situation ③

Mitch Vance gets an email from the Trinity Hotel asking him to evaluate its services. Read it and see if the results are positive or negative.

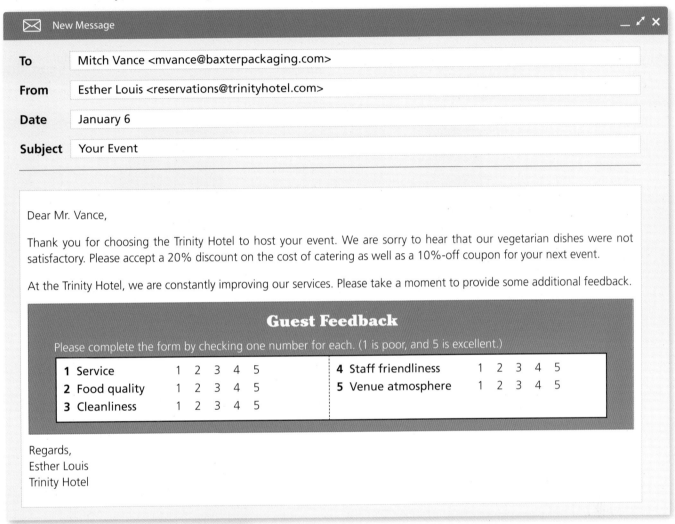

	New Message	_ ↗ ×
To	Mitch Vance <mvance@baxterpackaging.com>	
From	Esther Louis <reservations@trinityhotel.com>	
Date	January 6	
Subject	Your Event	

Dear Mr. Vance,

Thank you for choosing the Trinity Hotel to host your event. We are sorry to hear that our vegetarian dishes were not satisfactory. Please accept a 20% discount on the cost of catering as well as a 10%-off coupon for your next event.

At the Trinity Hotel, we are constantly improving our services. Please take a moment to provide some additional feedback.

Guest Feedback

Please complete the form by checking one number for each. (1 is poor, and 5 is excellent.)

1 Service	1 2 3 4 5		**4** Staff friendliness	1 2 3 4 5
2 Food quality	1 2 3 4 5		**5** Venue atmosphere	1 2 3 4 5
3 Cleanliness	1 2 3 4 5			

Regards,
Esther Louis
Trinity Hotel

Business English Dos and Don'ts

When responding to a customer complaint, there are a few ways to satisfy the customer. Apologize for the problem. Don't get defensive, and don't deny there was a problem.

Dos
- ○ We are sorry to hear that our vegetarian dishes were not satisfactory. (*apologetic*)
- ○ Please accept our sincere apologies. (*apologetic*)

Don'ts
- ✕ Actually, our vegetarian dishes are delicious. (*defensive*)
- ✕ Well, we didn't do anything wrong. (*denying*)

Offer compensation for mistakes in a professional manner without being resentful.

Dos
- ○ Please accept a 20% discount. (*professional*)
- ○ We'd like to offer you a coupon for your next event. (*professional*)

Don'ts
- ✕ I guess I have to offer you a discount. (*resentful*)
- ✕ Maybe a coupon will make you happy. (*resentful*)

Situation ❶

Ⓐ Andreas Webber asks for help filling out an expense report for his business trip. Read the conversation. 🔊 12-1

A Hi, Katherine. I went to Boston on business. I have to fill out an expense report, but I've never done that before. Can you help me?

K Sure. Did you fly there?

A Yes. The flight total was $506.78. I also spent $120 on taxis.

K Okay. Flight information is labeled airfare, and taxi fare is labeled transportation.

A How about my hotel expenses? My room charge was $478.87.

K That's labeled lodging. Did you take any clients to lunch or dinner?

A Yes, there were three dinners. I paid with my credit card.

K Write each one as a separate expense. Then, label them as meals.

A Okay, done.

K It looks good except you forgot to add the dates.

A Oh, right. The trip was from October 10 to 13.

K That was almost two months ago. We only have a month to submit expense reports.

A Oh, no. I had no idea.

K Speak to the accounting manager. Since it was your first trip, he may make an allowance.

Pop-up Questions

1 Where did Mr. Webber go on business?

2 How much did Mr. Webber spend on taxis?

3 How many dinners did Mr. Webber pay for?

4 Who will Mr. Webber likely contact next?

B **Take Notes ::** Based on the conversation in A, complete the expense report.

Date	Description	Category	Amount ($)	Payment Method
Submitted By: Andreas Webber				Submitted On: December 7
October 10	1	2	506.78	personal credit card
October 10-12	Hotel room (three nights)	3	478.87	personal credit card
October 10	Dinner with a client	Meals	153.88	4 ....
October 11	Dinner with a client	Meals	155.43	personal credit card
October 12	Dinner with a client	Meals	98.33	personal credit card
October 11-13	5	Transportation	6	cash
				Trip Total: $1,513.29

Background Knowledge

A Read and learn about business trip expense reports.

Many employees travel on business. You may attend expositions or conferences. You might meet new clients. Traveling on business can be expensive. Usually, your company will pay the bill. However, you must fill out an expense report before you can get reimbursed.

An expense report is a detailed chart that lists all of your expenses. It includes the date, description, and amount of each expense. It also mentions how the expense was paid, either by credit card or in cash. Each expense needs a category, such as airfare, lodging, or meals. This is important because some expenses are taxed differently when the company files its yearly taxes.

When you finish filling out your report, submit it to the Accounting Department. Make sure to submit it before the deadline. Your company will pay you back for your expenses. The payment might be included in your next paycheck.

Pop-up Questions

1 What does an expense report list?

2 Why does each expense need a category?

B Listen to conversation and answer the questions. 12-2

1 **Who went on the business trip?**

a. Julia and Henry   b. Julia and Maxwell   c. Henry and Maxwell

2 **What did Julia forget to add?**

a. the airfare   b. some dates   c. a taxi fare

3 **How many meals did Julia pay for?**

a. one   b. four   c. six

Vocabulary

A **Look at the pictures and learn some words related to business trips.**

Types of Expenses

 airfare

 lodging

 meals

 transportation

Words Related to Expense Reports

 expense report

colour, gloss	$0.08	500	$40.00

Subtotal	$370.00
Taxes	$23.85
Shipping	$10.00
Discount	-$0.00
Total	$403.85

ped in blue wrapping
ed saying, "Happy

subtotal

 deadline

```
          RECEIPT
Terminal#1    01-02-2018   11:32AM

1 x T-Shirt              $25.50
1 x Watches             $299.00
1 x Pants                $32.99
1 x Socks                 $6.50

TOTAL AMOUNT            $363.99
CASH                   $400.00
CHANGE                  $36.01

Bank Card       **** **** **** 7211
Approval#              192107

********* THANK YOU! *********
```

receipt

 credit card

cash

B **Complete the sentences with the words in the box.**

subtotal	airfare	expense report	credit card	receipt	meals	cash

1 She used a(n) _____ to book the hotel online.

2 The flight _____ is $503.68 before taxes.

3 Can you ask the waiter for a(n) _____ when you pay?

4 He doesn't usually carry much _____ in his wallet.

5 There were four items labeled as _____ in the report.

6 You should submit your _____ to the Accounting Department.

7 He flew first class, so his _____ cost over $2,000.

Speak Up

Practice the conversation with your partner by using the information on each expense report. 🔊 12-3

(Example)

expense report

Submitted By: George Drake

Date	Description	Category	Amount ($)	Payment Method
September 3	Return flight to Detroit	Airfare	489.54	personal credit card
September 3-5	Hotel room (two nights)	Lodging	398.23	personal credit card
September 3	Dinner with a client	Meals	87.44	cash
September 4	Dinner with a client	Meals	83.25	personal credit card

A Hi, Jen. Can you help me fill out my expense report?

B Sure, George. When was the trip?

A It was from September 3 to 5.

B Write that here. How much was your flight?

A It was $489.54.

B Write that here and label it as airfare.

A Okay. How about my meals?

B How many meals did you pay for?

A Well, I took two clients to dinner. Each meal was under $90.

B Write each one as an expense and include the exact cost.

! Tips for Success

When you fill out an expense report, add the exact cost for each expense. Don't round the number up or down.

(Expense Report 1)

Submitted By: Samuel Kim

Date	Description	Category	Amount ($)	Payment Method
June 4-5	Hotel room (one night)	Lodging	342.10	personal credit card
June 4	Lunch with a client	Meals	65.49	personal credit card
June 5	Lunch with a client	Meals	68.40	personal credit card
June 4	Taxi fare	Transportation	40.00	Cash

(Expense Report 2)

Submitted By: Claudia Wexler

Date	Description	Category	Amount ($)	Payment Method
February 15	Return flight to Sydney	Airfare	1,304.22	personal credit card
February 15-19	Hotel room (four nights)	Lodging	898.55	personal credit card
February 16	Dinner with a client	Meals	98.33	personal credit card
February 17	Dinner with a client	Meals	96.54	personal credit card

A **Let's learn about imperative sentences.**

Positive	Negative
Use **infinitive without "to"** to give orders, instructions, warnings, or advice and to make invitations.	Use **do not/don't + infinitive without "to"** to give orders, instructions, warnings, or advice.
Turn on the heater. It's cold in here.	**Don't open** the window. It's cold in here.
Write each one as a separate expense.	**Don't write** your meals as one expense.
Come in and **have** some coffee.	**Don't use** that cup! It's dirty.

B **Complete the sentences with the words in the box. Make the sentence negative if it's indicated in the parentheses.**

include	lose	reserve	sit	close	watch	meet	use

1 _____ that hotel room. It's much too small. (not)

2 _____ the amount of each expense in your report.

3 _____ out! The floor is wet. You might fall.

4 _____ these folders. They contain important documents. (not)

5 _____ that printer. It doesn't have any ink. (not)

6 _____ us at the restaurant. We will have lunch there.

7 _____ there! That bench is covered with wet paint. (not)

8 _____ the window. It's getting chilly in here.

Know-how *at Work*   **How to Collect Receipts**

It is important to collect receipts when you are on a business trip. Receipts prove the amounts you will list on your expense report. If you don't have a receipt, you might not get reimbursed for that expense.

1 Before you travel, you should book a flight and a hotel room. Print your electronic receipt. Keep it somewhere safe, such as in an envelope or in a desk drawer.

2 While traveling, get into the habit of asking for receipts. If you take a client out to dinner, ask the restaurant for a receipt. If you pay for gas, taxis, or admission into an event, get receipts for those expenses as well.

3 It's easy to lose receipts while traveling. Carry a folder or envelope with you. Put all your receipt inside it.

4 When you return from your business trip, fill out an expense report. Include your receipts in an envelope. If you send your report via email, scan all your receipts. Attach the scans to your email.

Situation 2

A Andreas Webber sends his expense report along with some scanned receipts to the accounting manager. Read the email.

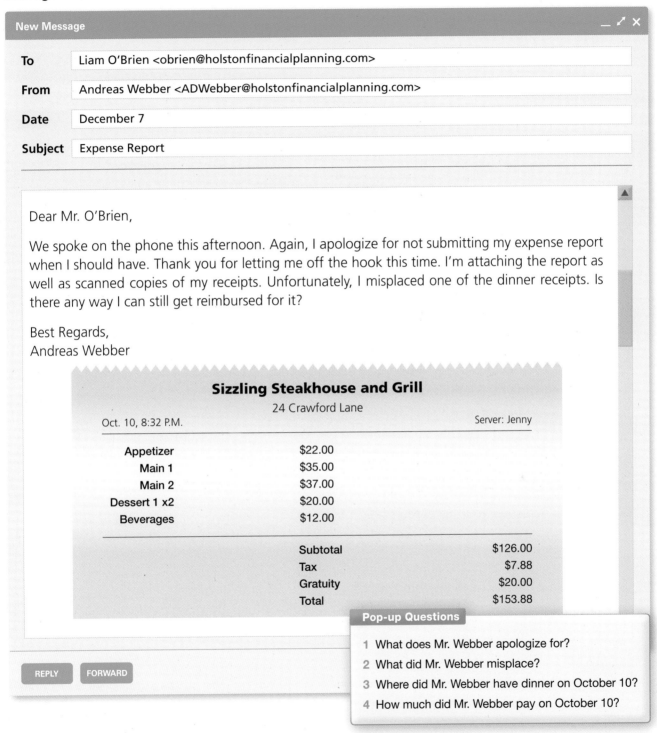

New Message   — ↗ ✕

To	Liam O'Brien <obrien@holstonfinancialplanning.com>
From	Andreas Webber <ADWebber@holstonfinancialplanning.com>
Date	December 7
Subject	Expense Report

Dear Mr. O'Brien,

We spoke on the phone this afternoon. Again, I apologize for not submitting my expense report when I should have. Thank you for letting me off the hook this time. I'm attaching the report as well as scanned copies of my receipts. Unfortunately, I misplaced one of the dinner receipts. Is there any way I can still get reimbursed for it?

Best Regards,
Andreas Webber

Sizzling Steakhouse and Grill
24 Crawford Lane

Oct. 10, 8:32 P.M.   Server: Jenny

Appetizer	$22.00
Main 1	$35.00
Main 2	$37.00
Dessert 1 x2	$20.00
Beverages	$12.00

Subtotal	$126.00
Tax	$7.88
Gratuity	$20.00
Total	$153.88

REPLY   FORWARD

Pop-up Questions

1 What does Mr. Webber apologize for?
2 What did Mr. Webber misplace?
3 Where did Mr. Webber have dinner on October 10?
4 How much did Mr. Webber pay on October 10?

B **Problem Solving ::** Andreas Webber gets a call from Liam O'Brien explaining that Andreas should also submit paper copies of his receipts. Find a partner and choose the roles of Andreas Webber and Liam O'Brien. Then, role-play to discuss a possible solution. Use the information from the email in A if necessary.

A **Let's learn some expressions to use in business.**

When explaining an action via email	When asking that something be done via email
I'm attaching the report as well as scanned copies of my receipts.	Can you attach your report as well as scanned copies of your receipts?
I'm forwarding you the invitation to the conference.	Could you forward me the invitation to the conference?
I have pasted the event program below.	Can you email me the event program?
I attached the report to my previous email.	If you haven't sent the report yet, please do so.
When continuing a conversation	**When mentioning that something is lost**
We spoke on the phone this afternoon.	Unfortunately, I misplaced one of the dinner receipts.
I emailed you about a customer yesterday.	Sadly, I can't seem to find the folder.
As I mentioned in the breakroom, we need to submit the report.	It seems the package never arrived at her office.

B **Fill in the blanks with the correct answers from the box. Then, practice the conversation with a partner.** 🔊 12-4

> it seems some of your receipts are missing   I'm emailing the credit card receipt to you now
> I misplaced one of the lunch receipts   we spoke on the phone this afternoon

A Hi. This is Wesley from Accounting. [1]_____.

B Hi, Wesley. Did you get my expense report?

A Yes, I'm looking at it now. [2]_____.

B Oh, right. Unfortunately, [3]_____.

A Yes, you mentioned that on the phone.

B Is something else missing?

A Well, you attached your hotel reservation but not the receipt.

B Oh, my mistake. [4]_____.

A Thanks.

B Let me know if you need anything else.

A Everything else looks good. I'll add the amount to your next paycheck.

Extra Practice

Role-play with your partner. One person mentions a receipt is missing. The other person explains that the receipt was lost.

A Hi. We spoke on the phone yesterday.

B Right. Did you get my expense report?

A Yes. It seems your car rental receipt is missing.

B Unfortunately, I misplaced it.

Situation ③

Andreas Webber gets a reply from Liam O'Brien detailing how much money will be reimbursed. Read the email and see if the results are positive or negative.

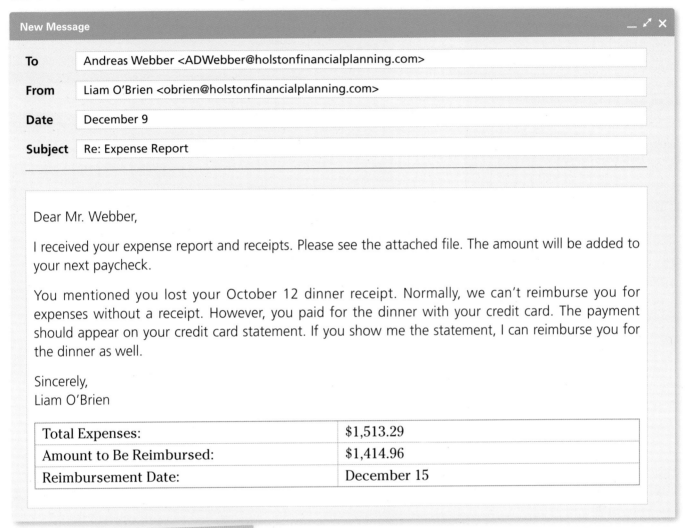

New Message	— ↗ ✕
To	Andreas Webber <ADWebber@holstonfinancialplanning.com>
From	Liam O'Brien <obrien@holstonfinancialplanning.com>
Date	December 9
Subject	Re: Expense Report

Dear Mr. Webber,

I received your expense report and receipts. Please see the attached file. The amount will be added to your next paycheck.

You mentioned you lost your October 12 dinner receipt. Normally, we can't reimburse you for expenses without a receipt. However, you paid for the dinner with your credit card. The payment should appear on your credit card statement. If you show me the statement, I can reimburse you for the dinner as well.

Sincerely,
Liam O'Brien

Total Expenses:	$1,513.29
Amount to Be Reimbursed:	$1,414.96
Reimbursement Date:	December 15

Business English Dos and Don'ts

When you are helping a coworker complete an expense report, there are a few things to remember. Be specific about the course of action your coworker must take.

Dos
- ○ If you show me the statement, I can reimburse you for the dinner. (*specific*)
- ○ Send scanned copies of your receipts by Friday. (*specific*)

Don'ts
- ✕ Maybe a statement would be useful. (*vague*)
- ✕ Hand in the receipts soon, please. (*vague*)

Mention company regulations and procedures in a clear and professional manner.

Dos
- ○ Normally, we can't reimburse you for expenses without a receipt. (*professional*)
- ○ Include the exact cost of each expense. (*clear*)

Don'ts
- ✕ It's silly, but that's the company's policy. (*unprofessional*)
- ✕ You should include all the information. (*unclear*)

Answer Key

Mission 01 | Preparing for a Meeting

Situation ❶

A

1 He will bring four people.
2 He wants to reserve Conference Room A.
3 He requested a projector.
4 He wants to order pastries.

B

1 Price Shipping
3 Conference
5 tech support
7 tea

2 July 28 / 10:00 A.M.
4 Twenty
6 coffee
8 pastries

Background Knowledge

A

1 People discuss many items related to business, such as sales figures, marketing plans, and budgets.
2 Video conferences

B

> W Hi, Jeff. This is Wanda calling. I heard you have a meeting next week. Are you still using the conference room for it?
>
> M I planned to originally, but Ms. West is unable to travel to our office. I might set up a conference call instead.
>
> W How about a video conference? The company just installed a video conferencing system on the first floor.
>
> M Oh, really? That's a great idea.
>
> W Just call Max in tech support. He can help you get started.

1 c   2 b   3 b

Vocabulary

B

1 microphone
2 speakers
3 monitor
4 brainstorming area
5 speakerphone
6 theater
7 video-conferencing camera
8 whiteboard and markers

GRAMMAR

1 will get

2 am going to write
3 are going to tour
4 will call
5 will cancel
6 are not going to buy

Situation ❷

A

1 It has already been booked.
2 He suggests the theater first.
3 It only has 15 chairs.
4 She asks him to check if the project works.

Useful Expressions

1 I'd like to reserve a room
2 I don't think that will work
3 That will have to do
4 can you check if the projector works

Mission 02 | Giving Directions

Situation ❶

A

1 It's a new building.
2 It will take him to the waterfront.
3 He should turn left.
4 It's the tallest in the area.

B

1 three
3 waterfront
5 warehouses

2 right
4 left
6 restaurants

Background Knowledge

A

1 You can give verbal directions.
2 A screenshot of a map

B

> M Hi, Sally. I just got a message from Robert. He needs directions to the office.
>
> W Sure, Brandon. Where is he right now?
>
> M He said he's at the Plaza, but I have no idea where that is.

W Oh, I know that place. It's a brand-new theater just a few blocks away. It used to be a department store.

M Ah, okay, I know where he is then. He needs to turn right on First Avenue, go three blocks, and then turn left onto Jackson Drive.

W That's right.

1 c   **2** b   **3** b

Vocabulary

1 traffic light   **2** dead end

3 one-way street   **4** waterfront

5 crosswalk   **6** traffic circle

7 alley   **8** blocks

GRAMMAR

1 across from

2 on

3 next to / by

4 on the corner of

5 across from

Situation ❷

Ⓐ

1 It is being serviced.

2 Her department is having a meeting.

3 It is next to the restrooms.

4 He needs a key.

Useful Expressions

1 Where are you now

2 Could you give me directions

3 Go south and turn right onto King Street

4 Which street do I turn onto

Mission 03 Picking Up a Client at the Airport

Situation ❶

Ⓐ

1 She will discuss the distribution of her new clothing line.

2 She departs on February 7.

3 She's flying to New York.

4 He got the arrival time wrong.

Ⓑ

1 London   **2** ZF83

3 10:25 A.M.   **4** New York

5 1:05 P.M.

Background Knowledge

Ⓐ

1 You should hold a sign with the client's name written on it.

2 The client's bag

Ⓑ

W Steve, I heard you're picking up Mr. Vangaras at the airport tomorrow. Have you ever picked up a client before?

M No, Jenny, I haven't. Do you have any tips?

W It's important to be on time. Check the arrival time and get there about thirty minutes early.

M If the flight is delayed, I might be waiting around for an hour or more.

W You might. But don't mention it to the client. Instead, ask him about his flight. Be as friendly as possible.

1 a   **2** a   **3** b

Vocabulary

Ⓑ

1 baggage claim

2 gate

3 check-in desk

4 airport security

5 car rental booth

6 currency exchange booth

7 departures

8 duty-free shop

GRAMMAR

1 showed   **2** heard

3 broke   **4** paid

5 asked   **6** picked

7 drove   **8** called

Situation ❷

Ⓐ

1 There was a snowstorm.

2 She asks to delay the meeting by a day.

3 She was planning to fly to L.A.

4 The driver will take her to a hotel.

1 my flight has been canceled

2 I won't be able to attend the meeting

3 I'm sorry to hear that

4 I would appreciate that

04 | Ordering Office Supplies

Situation ❶

1 He wants to order 12 boxes.

2 The ink smeared during printing.

3 He wants to order file folders and folder labels.

4 The security guard receives deliveries.

1 Jan Temple	**2** A4 Paper
3 12	**4** Letter Size
5 Labels	**6** 1

Background Knowledge

Ⓐ

1 You should take an inventory of the supplies currently in the office.

2 Most orders are now placed online.

Ⓑ

> M Hi, Lin. This is Walter from Accounting.
>
> W Hi, Walter. How can I help you?
>
> M I heard you're ordering office supplies this week. Can you add ink cartridges to your list? I also need three boxes of paper.
>
> W Actually, Michelle is going to order the supplies this time. Can you compile a list for your department and give it to her?
>
> M Oh, sure. No problem. Do you know when she needs the list by?
>
> W I think she's going to call the supply company with the order this Friday.

1 a   **2** c   **3** b

Vocabulary

Ⓑ

1 staples   **2** envelope

3 notepad   **4** correction tape

5 toner   **6** staple remover

7 binder   **8** ink cartridge

1 am sending	**2** is going
3 is calling	**4** are having
5 are working	**6** is opening
7 are staying	**8** is having

Situation ❷

1 It is a popular item.

2 She asks her to send one box of paper.

3 She does not want the X-Com Brand.

4 She will send it on April 15.

1 How can I help you

2 Let me check your account

3 Would you like to order a different brand

4 Would you like me to rush the delivery

05 | Applying for a Training Session

Situation ❶

Ⓐ

1 They received it this morning.

2 She will apply for the social media management workshop.

3 She was promoted to team leader.

4 She suggests they carpool.

Ⓑ

1 Leadership Training

2 auditorium 1

3 October 20

4 10:00 A.M. to 4:00 P.M.

5 next Thursday

6 Social Media Management

7 auditorium 2

8 October 20

9 10:00 A.M. to 3:00 P.M.

10 next Friday

Background Knowledge

A

1 They often go through an orientation period.

2 Technical skills training

B

> **M** Hi, Jenny. Are you going to attend the winter training program next week?
>
> **W** Yes, I'll be at our head office on Wednesday for technical skills training. I wanted to take social media management, but it runs at the same time.
>
> **M** Right. I guess I won't see you there then.
>
> **W** Aren't you taking any classes this year?
>
> **M** Mine are on Thursday. Since we're launching new products next year, my entire team will take product and service training.
>
> **W** That's exciting. I hope you enjoy it.

1 a   **2** b   **3** c

Vocabulary

B

1 diversity   **2** conflict resolution

3 social media   **4** presentation

5 teamwork   **6** leadership

7 problem-solving   **8** time management

GRAMMAR

1 Should / meet   **2** should request

3 should email   **4** Should / apply

5 should hire   **6** should have

7 Should / reserve   **8** should carpool

Situation ❷

A

1 It runs all day on October 20.

2 He suggests taking some management classes.

3 The application deadline has passed.

4 Victoria Rogers is in charge of handling applications.

Useful Expressions

1 Certainly

2 I will ask her right away

3 It won't be any trouble

4 Fill me in when you can

Situation ❶

A

1 He is going to Hawaii.

2 She went to Paris last year.

3 It has an orientation session.

4 He was going to lead a warehouse tour.

B

1 Operations   **2** Jeffrey Black

3 Days   **4** June 15

5 June 26   **6** Vacation

Background Knowledge

A

1 You should note the reason you will be away.

2 This will help your company prepare for your absence.

B

> **W** Hello, Mr. West. This is Margaret calling. I just heard that my grandfather passed away last night. I emailed you my time-off request form, but I wanted to leave you a message as well. I have to leave after lunch today. I'm catching a late flight to California to attend the funeral. I'll be gone until next Wednesday. I spoke with Catherine in my department. She agreed to take over my workload while I'm away. In addition, if there are any problems, you can contact me by email. Thank you for understanding.

1 c   **2** a   **3** b

Vocabulary

B

1 medical   **2** wedding

3 bereavement   **4** paternity

5 voting   **6** vacation

7 military   **8** jury duty

GRAMMAR

1 will be conducting

2 Will you be speaking

3 will be traveling

4 will be showing

5 Will they be visiting

6 Will we be sharing

7 will be renovating

8 Will you be working

Situation ❷

Ⓐ

1 She says Mr. Black did a great job.

2 The manager approved it last week.

3 He will be there for two weeks.

4 He suggests Jim Walsh.

1 My doctor told me I need to have surgery

2 I'm positive she'd do a great job

3 Wonderful

4 I'm going to need your signature

Mission 07 | Dealing with a Customer's Inquiry

Situation ❶

Ⓐ

1 She is the district manager of Universal Fitness.

2 She was trying to call Mr. Peterson.

3 They are currently out of the office.

4 He will pass along a message to Mr. Peterson.

Ⓑ

1 Bob Peterson
2 Bethany Morton
3 Universal Fitness
4 district manager
5 clubs
6 energy drinks
7 Mathew Fernsby

Background Knowledge

Ⓐ

1 You should greet the customer politely.

2 You should thank the customer for calling.

Ⓑ

> **M** Hello. This is Joshua Black calling from Urban Style T-Shirts. I've seen your company's fall sweater designs, and I'd like to sell them at my shop.
>
> **W** Actually, this is Tessa White from Human Resources. Are you trying to reach Tim in Sales?
>
> **M** Yes, sorry. Can you connect me with him?
>
> **W** Unfortunately, Tim is off today. I can deliver a message to him if you like.

> **M** That would be great. Have him call me back at 444-098-9922.
>
> **W** Thank you and have a lovely day.

1 a   **2** a   **3** b

Vocabulary

Ⓑ

1 c   **2** e   **3** a
4 g   **5** d   **6** f
7 b   **8** h

1 talked, quitting

2 objected, working

3 were, spending

4 was, applying

5 apologized, being

6 worried, getting

7 was, sending

8 believed, rewarding

Situation ❷

Ⓐ

1 He's meeting some clients.

2 He was planning to deliver it tomorrow.

3 He thinks Universal Fitness could be a big client.

4 He will call her on the phone.

1 How are you doing

2 How about you

3 Not bad. Thanks

4 I apologize for the interruption

Mission 08 | Asking for Some Repairs

Situation ❶

Ⓐ

1 The copy machine is broken again.

2 He's scheduled to come tomorrow at 2:00 P.M.

3 She needs to copy some contracts.

4 She might have to go to the copy store.

B

1 jammed   **2** smears

3 tomorrow   **4** afternoon

5 today

Background Knowledge

A

1 They can damage electronic equipment quickly.

2 You should make sure to clean it thoroughly.

B

W	Oh, no. My computer is broken again.
M	What's the matter with it?
W	It keeps overheating and shutting off. I think the fans inside are dirty.
M	Well, the repairman is coming to update all the computers this Sunday. Can it wait until then?
W	Actually, I have a big report due this evening. I really need to finish it and print it.
M	I'll call him to see if he can stop by today. Otherwise, you might have to retype the report on another computer.

1 c   **2** b   **3** a

Vocabulary

B

1 b   **2** d   **3** c

4 a   **5** e

C

1 air conditioner   **2** copy machine

3 heater   **4** tablet

5 paper shredder

GRAMMAR

1 is broken   **2** were delivered

3 Were, made   **4** was not saved

5 Was, cleaned   **6** was approved

7 Is, interested   **8** was not fixed

Situation ❷

A

1 She works at the Grove Employment Agency.

2 She asks him to stop by today.

3 He will visit at 4:00 P.M. today.

4 He says it's an old model.

Useful Expressions

1 I don't suppose you could fix it today

2 Sorry, but my schedule is full today

3 If my memory serves me right

4 Yes, that's correct

Mission 09   Sending a Sample

Situation ❶

A

1 She opened a tutoring business.

2 She teaches math and geography.

3 He recommends *Learning Scape*.

4 She asks him to send a sample of each book.

B

1 5   **2** Geography

3 Beginner   **4** 3

5 Priya Jain

Background Knowledge

A

1 They help businesses choose which products to sell.

2 Sellers must remember to mark the products.

B

M	Hi, Joshua. This is William from Sales. I just got off the phone with a potential customer, Jane Murphey. She just opened a new clothing shop called Jane's Boutique downtown, and I'd like to send her some samples. Can you put together a box for me? I want to include everything from our fall women's line. One item each in medium should do. Don't forget to include an invoice as well, but don't charge her for the samples. And please make sure to mark the items.

1 c   **2** b   **3** a

Vocabulary

A

1 logo   **2** zip code

3 client address   **4** description

5 quantity   **6** unit price

7 total

B

1 invoice
2 unit price
3 total
4 client address
5 description

GRAMMAR

1 Who
2 When
3 Where
4 Whose
5 Which
6 What
7 How
8 Why

Situation ❷

A

1 She likes the layout of *Learning Scape*.
2 She orders fifteen copies of level 2.
3 It is too difficult for her sixth graders.
4 She asks him to send some more samples.

Useful Expressions

1 You've reached Curtains Unlimited
2 Can I put you on hold for a minute
3 my customers especially love pastel colors
4 Understood

Mission 10 | Preparing for a Business Trip

Situation ❶

A

1 He was invited to the international business conference.
2 Kit Patterson and Janet Hunter will go.
3 It is in Los Angeles.
4 They can register on a website.

B

1 potential clients
2 July 10 to 13
3 West Exhibition Center in Los Angeles
4 Janet Hunter
5 flights and hotel rooms

Background Knowledge

A

1 If it gets delayed, you might have to wait until the next day to travel.
2 Checked luggage might get lost.

B

> W Hello, Frederick. This is Molly from Management.
>
> M Hi, Molly. How are you?
>
> W Great. Thank you. I just received an invitation to the London Businessperson of the Year Gala. I would like you and Janice in Sales to attend the event with me.
>
> M We'd be happy to. When is it?
>
> W It's in London at the Grand Valley Resort on December 10.
>
> M Okay. I'll book us three seats on a flight to London. I'll call the resort and see if it has rooms available, too.
>
> W If not, try the Holiday Hotel. It has great reviews online.

1 a
2 a
3 b

Vocabulary

B

1 attend a meeting
2 business card
3 luggage
4 rent a car
5 Get a receipt
6 charger
7 book a hotel room
8 boarding pass

GRAMMAR

1 shocked
2 worried
3 boring
4 challenging
5 disappointing
6 inspiring
7 depressed
8 impressed

Situation ❷

A

1 There was a fire there last week.
2 The repairs will not be done in time.
3 They should go to the East Exhibition Center.
4 It is from July 9 to 12.

Useful Expressions

1 I'm calling to let you know about some changes
2 Sadly, we had to change the date
3 I hope you can still attend
4 I'm sincerely sorry for the inconvenience

Mission 11 — Holding a Work Party

Situation ❶

A

1 He reserves the banquet room.
2 Ms. Prince will take photos during the event.
3 He will be on vacation then.
4 It will take place on December 27.

B

1 Year-end
2 December 27 / 6:00 to 11:00 P.M.
3 122
4 vegetarian and gluten-free
5 event program
6 Set up the audio equipment

Background Knowledge

A

1 Events help employees celebrate successes and help build professional relationships.
2 The date, the time, and the dress code

B

> M Hi, Oliver. This is Christopher Marshall calling. I heard you planned our last fundraiser, so I was wondering if you could organize another event. Rochelle Vincente in your department is retiring this year. I'd like you to plan a dinner party for her in April. It should include your department and the office managers, so there will be 18 people in total. A restaurant would be best. Choose one that has vegetarian options. We should also get a retirement gift for Ms. Vincente. Please ask Barbara Fields to handle that. Let me know if you have any questions. Thanks, Oliver.

1 b	2 a	3 c

Vocabulary

B

1 e	2 h	3 b
4 a	5 f	6 c
7 g	8 d	

GRAMMAR

1 to send	2 to ask
3 to make	4 to choose
5 to rent	6 to walk
7 to interrupt	8 to get

Situation ❷

A

1 He works for Baxter Packaging.
2 122 guests will attend the event.
3 He requested gluten-free and vegetarian options.
4 He can call Esther Louis.

Useful Expressions

1 Thank you for choosing the Westhill Resort
2 we offer a wide variety of catering options
3 Please keep it as confirmation
4 If you'd like to make any other changes

Mission 12 — Asking for Expense Reimbursement

Situation ❶

A

1 He went to Boston.
2 He spent $120 on taxis.
3 He paid for three dinners.
4 He will contact the accounting manager.

B

1 Flight
2 Airfare
3 Lodging
4 personal credit card
5 Taxi fare
6 120.00

Background Knowledge

A

1 It lists all of your expenses.
2 Some expenses are taxed differently when the company files its yearly taxes.

B

> M Hi, Julia. I got your expense report from the business trip you took with Maxwell. You forgot to fill out a few things.
> W Oh, I did? Sorry, Henry. Which part did I forget?
> M Well, you didn't add the dates of your hotel stay. You also included all your meals as one expense.
> W I see. How should I fill out that part?

M Each meal is its own expense.

W Oh, so I have to write down six different expenses for that?

M That's correct. Make sure to submit a receipt for each meal as well.

1 b   **2** b   **3** c

Vocabulary

B

1 credit card   **2** subtotal

3 receipt   **4** cash

5 meals   **6** expense report

7 airfare

GRAMMAR

1 Don't reserve   **2** Include

3 Watch   **4** Don't lose

5 Don't use   **6** Meet

7 Don't sit   **8** Close

Situation ❷

A

1 He apologizes for not submitting his expense report.

2 He misplaced one of the dinner receipts.

3 He had dinner at the Sizzling Steakhouse and Grill.

4 He paid $153.88.

Useful Expressions

1 We spoke on the phone this afternoon

2 It seems some of your receipts are missing

3 I misplaced one of the lunch receipts

4 I'm emailing the credit card receipt to you now